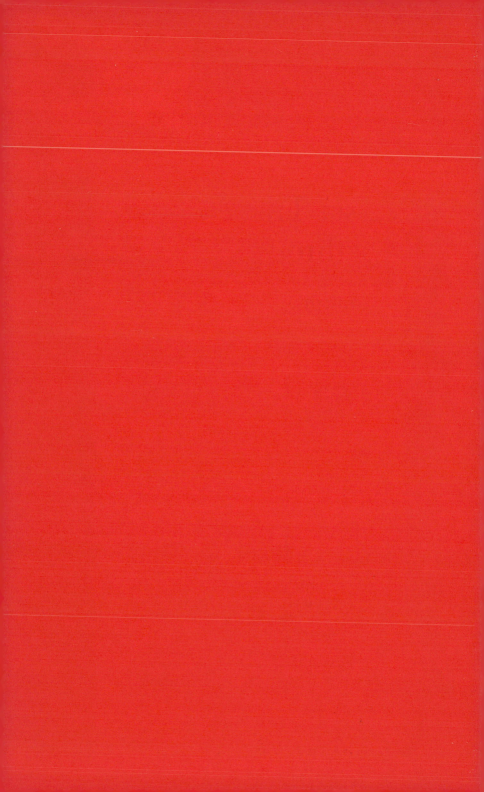

Russia Transformed: Breakthrough to Hope

Moscow, August 1991

James H. Billington

THE FREE PRESS
A Division of Macmillan, Inc.
NEW YORK
Maxwell Macmillan Canada
TORONTO
Maxwell Macmillan International
NEW YORK   OXFORD   SINGAPORE   SYDNEY

The Free Press
A Division of Macmillan, Inc.
866 Third Avenue, New York, N.Y. 10022

Maxwell Macmillan Canada, Inc.
1200 Eglinton Avenue East
Suite 200
Don Mills, Ontario M3C 3N1

Macmillan, Inc. is part of the Maxwell Communication Group of Companies.

Printed in the United States of America

printing number
1 2 3 4 5 6 7 8 9 10

Library of Congress Cataloging-in-Publication Data

Billington, James H.
    Russia transformed—breakthrough to hope : Moscow, August 1991 / James H. Billington.
       p. cm.
    Includes index.
    ISBN 0–02–903515–5
    1. Soviet Union—History—Attempted coup, 1991—Personal narratives, American. 2. Billington, James H. I. Title.
DK292.B55 1992
947.085′4—dc20   92–24944
                                      CIP

We always had faith and love,
now we have hope.

—*Old woman at the barricades*
Moscow, August 21, 1991

CONTENTS

CONTENTS

PART FOUR
FORCES OF RENEWAL

PART FIVE
RETROSPECT AND PROSPECT

PART ONE

Introduction

The events of August 1991 in Moscow may in time be recognized to have been the most important single political happening of the second half of the twentieth century. During the decisive forty-eight hours from the early morning of August 19 to the early morning of August 21, the most destructive ideology and powerful empire of our time fell apart—and the hitherto largely passive and divided Russian people came together.

Suddenly confronted with a putsch that reimposed from the top down the old Leninist politics of fear, Russians unexpectedly found a way to affirm a new politics of hope. They defended on exposed barricades, in a near-steady rain, the site of their first democratically elected government, the now famous White House of the Russian Republic, which replaced the imperial Kremlin as the locus of legitimacy for the Russian people.

This was the decisive break with the totalitarian system that had continued to paralyze inner feelings long after its outer controls had weakened. Stalin had called 1929, the year when he plunged the Soviet Union into the horror of forced collectivization, "the year of the great break," using the word *perelom*, which suggests severing a bone, or the break in a fever determining whether a patient lives or dies. A comparable break had begun in 1989, sixty years later, when a surprising series of mostly peaceful popular upheavals ended Communist rule in the Soviet outer empire in Eastern Europe. That wave of change reached the Soviet

Union's own national minorities in 1990, and Russia itself in 1991.

The Cold War ended with neither a bang nor a whimper, but with the unanticipated, spontaneous heroism of a relatively small band of Russians at the heart of empire in Moscow. These events provided an adrenalin shot of hope and self-confidence to the Russian people. But soaring summer hopes predictably gave way to a winter of discontent, for the events started in motion a process of innovation and change in Russian society that was bound to continue in conditions fraught with peril.

Democracy was an endangered species even at birth, threatened by ethnic and economic problems that seemed destined to get even worse before they could start getting better. The post-Communist Russian commitment to democracy and a market economy was not accompanied by any real historical experience in Russia or exposure to functioning foreign institutions. Their preparation for a new path was inadequate, and many zigzags clearly still lay ahead.

Yet the Russian people were transformed psychologically by the events of August. They acquired a new sense of their own creative potential for remaking their country from the bottom up. With the destruction of the most powerful political machine of the twentieth century, the Soviet Communist Party and its police structure, the way was opened for ordinary people to participate in, and have some chance to affect, the political, economic, and spiritual life of their nation. The remarkably nonutopian objective was to create a "normal" society and to become part of the "civilized" world.

To understand the immensity of the change that the August days brought to Russia, one must recall the heavy legacy of Russian history, with its almost unrelieved record of autocratic rule and popular submissiveness.

1

The Legacy of Russian History

The political history of Russia begins (as recorded in the twelfth-century *Primary Chronicle*) with the Russian people imploring a foreign prince (Rurik) in the ninth century to send them rulers to bring order to their unruly land. Everything of importance subsequently seems to have come from the top down: Prince Vladimir's conversion to Orthodox Christianity in the late tenth century, Peter the Great's opening of Russia to the West in the early eighteenth, Stalin's forced industrialization of the 1930s, and even Gorbachev's *perestroika*.

Political rule in Russia became more autocratic as it became more extensive. The exposed position of the Eastern Slavs on the unprotected eastern plains of Europe, the so-called steppe, required a strong military force, which became the key institution of the Russian realm. The long Mongol occupation began only a little more than a century after the Eastern Slavs had accepted Byzantine civilization and left a despotic legacy in Russia. The capital moved north into the forest: from Kiev on a river leading West to the Mediterranean, to Moscow on a river leading to the Caspian Sea and Asia.

The rising Muscovite Tsars threw off the Mongol yoke in the fifteenth century but often resembled their former overlords more than the relatively placid late emperors of Byzantium. When Constantinople fell to the Turks in 1453, Moscow blamed the decadence of the "Second Rome" and claimed to have become the "Third Rome," the apocalyptic final empire of Christian history. Under Tsar Ivan IV, "the Terrible," in the mid-sixteenth century Russia launched aggressive wars both east and west, adding to Russia for the first time territory that had not previously been part of the original patrimony of Kievan Rus.

During the next three centuries, Russian power slowly but steadily expanded northeast across Siberia to Alaska, southeast across vast regions of inner Asia, southwest to the Black Sea, and northwest along the Baltic Sea. A state was improvised to rule over what became by the nineteenth century the largest contiguous land empire in the history of the world. The imperial administration was, not surprisingly, based on the same principles of hierarchy and discipline as the army. The key institutions were the European world's most absolute monarch, the Tsar, and an ever larger political police force, beginning with Ivan the Terrible's *Oprichnina*, through the nineteenth-century *Okhrana* on to its multiple acronymic identities in Soviet times: CHEKA, OGPU, NKVD, KGB.

Ordinary Russians identified themselves by their Orthodox faith—the words Christian (*khristianin*) and peasant (*krestianin*) being almost identical in their traditional, rural society. But the ideology that was used to turn them periodically into cannon fodder was a negative nationalism derived from the traditional fears that exposed peoples on the steppe felt toward both external invaders and internal betrayal. Foreign emissaries were always thought to be coming into a steppe people's fortified citadel (kremlin) not to negotiate seriously, but to see how much ammunition and provisions were stored there to resist a siege. A series of conflicts with the West led to invasions: by the Poles in the early seventeenth century, the Swedes in the early eighteenth, the French in the early nineteenth, and the Germans twice in the twentieth. All were repelled by massive Russian resistance. The struggles both strengthened suspicions about foreigners and seemed to legitimize the existing autocracy.

At only two points in the late days of Tsarist rule—after 1855 and after 1905—did there seem to be any hope of opening up this relatively closed society to Western-style democratic and market institutions. Both times defeat in war opened this otherwise immovable colossus to the possibility of serious reform. After defeat in the Crimean War of 1853–55, Alexander II ended serfdom, introduced legal and local government reforms, and began a dramatic process of economic development. In the midst of losing a war with Japan in 1904–5, Nicholas II experimented with a kind of proto-parliament (the Duma) and abolished censorship for the first time in Russian history. Far from receiving the gratitude of their people, however, both Tsars were eventually murdered by Russian revolutionaries, who had taken on many of the characteristics of the hierarchical, militarized elite in the autocracy they were seeking to overthrow.

The resistance to absolute autocracy in this sprawling agrarian–military empire was not led, as in the West, by the urban, entrepreneurial classes. Industry and commerce were relatively backward and largely dominated by non-Russians (Germans, Swedes, Jews, Armenians). The resistance was dominated, instead, by ideological dissenters who tended to fight the official fanaticism of Tsardom with an even more virulent fanaticism of their own.

First came religious dissenters in the seventeenth and eighteenth centuries. Most extreme were the fundamentalists of the Muscovite Orthodox ritual, the apocalyptical Old Believers, who either burned themselves or withdrew to distant (and often very productive) communities in the deep interior of Russia to await the Last Judgment rather than cooperate with the Tsar-Antichrists. There was also a steady stream of sectarian offshoots of Protestantism who believed they could force their way into earthly perfection by discarding the rites of the Orthodox Church and purifying moral behavior. They called variously for fasts involving milk drinking (the *molokone*); "spirit-wrestling" resistance to external authority, including demonstrations of nudity (the *dukhobortsy*); seeking prophetic purity through flagellation (the *khlysty*); and even attaining angelic status through castration (the *skoptsy*).

This rich tradition believed that heaven could be realized on earth somewhere "by the white waters," presumably in the interior of Russia, and that the key to deliverance lay in some all-redeeming "heavenly book" (*Golubinaia Kniga*). The imperial censors' fear of subversive books became the hope of the secular intellectuals as they took over from religious dissenters in the nineteenth century the leadership of the opposition to Tsarist autocracy.

The famous Russian Intelligentsia tended to fight official dogmatism with an even more fanatical dogmatism of its own. The Russian revolutionary tradition was created by a small intellectual elite, which established its own secret hierarchies, ideological orthodoxies, and rituals of excommunication. Russians invented the word "terrorism" as a badge of pride[1] and focused at times obsessively on ritual political assassination and on capturing the instruments of power. With the arrival of Marxism, *Das Kapital* replaced the *Golubinaia Kniga* as the guide to an earthly utopia; the language of science replaced that of religion as the justification for exercising absolute power. After Lenin's authoritarian party consolidated power amid the war and revolutionary chaos of 1917, the Russian empire was reconsolidated under even more autocratic leadership. Moscow became the seat of the "Third International," a world Communist movement with far more universal pretensions than Moscow had ever projected as the "Third Rome."

Autocracy proved far more intrusive and all-permeating in the new Union of Soviet Socialist Republics than it had been in the mellowing empire of the Romanov Tsars. Joseph Stalin used Lenin's Bolshevik Party to build the world's first totalitarian state. He combined the worst features of reactionary xenophobia with a grotesque effort to realize an egalitarian utopia—and ended up killing more of his own people in peacetime than any political leader in recorded history. A series of Stalin's younger accomplices and protégés—Khrushchev, Brezhnev, Andropov, Chernenko—succeeded Stalin and institutionalized the totalitarian system of controls. Khrushchev rendered it acceptable to an anesthetized West by eliminating the largest part of the concentration camp system. But the empire grew steadily larger—extending overseas to new continents in Cuba, Vietnam, and Ethiopia—while internal opposition became ever more fragmented and isolated. Fear, it seemed, had been permanently embedded in the Russian personality.

Although some hopes were raised after the arrival in 1985 of Mikhail Gorbachev as the first leader of the post-Stalin generation, he rose to power strictly as a favored child of the totalitarian state's inner control system (the so-called *nomenklatura*) and seemed intent on launching only the kind of limited reform-from-above traditionally designed to strengthen rather than undermine central authority. Moreover, he steadily increased his own power through a series of political maneuvers even while allowing unprecedented freedom of speech (*glasnost*) and a measure of electoral choice in new parliamentary bodies. In late 1990 and early 1991 he reverted to autocratic form by appointing a host of conservative leaders to key government agencies, particularly in the internal security forces and the military–industrial complex, the bastions of totalitarian control.

It seemed inconceivable, therefore, in August 1991, that this tradition of autocracy fortified by modern mechanisms of control and terror could be overturned in a few days—least of all in Moscow itself, where both the instruments and the perquisites of power were available for their respective tasks of either coercing or co-opting potential opposition.

That the entire totalitarian structure should come apart so rapidly and decisively is one of those great mutations of history that defy traditional categories of explanation. It was exhilarating for me, as a historian who had studied Russia for nearly half a century, to be present for events that I knew from the beginning would be historic. I may have been no less enthusiastic about the transformations of August 1991 than John Reed was about those of October 1917. But I never saw myself as a journalist or a political activist. I did not, during the crucial events, seek entry into the key power centers of either the junta or the Yeltsin resistance. But I spent a great deal of time mingling in the streets and on the barricades, talking intensely with a wide variety of people for nearly a week. I got little sleep and took no photographs and only a few notes, yet I have a clearer recall of that week than of any other in my life. The country whose troubled culture I had first tried comprehensively to study twenty-five years ago in *The Icon and the Axe* was being convulsed before my very eyes by the kind of revolutionary upheaval I had written about ten years ago in *Fire in the Minds of Men*.

My perspective on these events reflects the two business capacities in which I had traveled to Moscow: as a representative of the Library of Congress to the annual congress of the International Federation of Library Associations and as almost the only person not of Russian origin at an unprecedented "Congress of Compatriots." The latter event was an ingathering of Russian emigrés invited back by the government of the Russian Republic to meet their "compatriots" summoned from all over the sprawling Russian Republic. Both of these congresses opened on August 19, the day the coup was launched. I was, therefore, in continuous contact throughout the crisis period with two groups particularly concerned with the cause of freedom: Russian librarians and provincial Russians sympathetic to Yeltsin.

Since knowledge is a key perquisite of power in a totalitarian state, the great libraries of the Soviet Union had always been under strict Party control. Much interesting material was not included in the public catalogues, and much more was isolated from any public use in "special repositories." Yet, because of the relative anonymity of library work, many serious scholars took refuge from persecution in libraries during the Soviet era and quietly preserved many books that police and censors tried to destroy. With the advent of glasnost, Russian librarians had begun to raise their voices in behalf of free access and an end to political controls.

As Librarian of Congress, I had joined the first American library delegation to the USSR in the summer of 1987, had hosted a return visit of Soviet librarians on the Fourth of July 1988, and had led an international effort to aid the Library of the Academy of Sciences in St. Petersburg after the largest fire in library history. We now conduct major exchange programs with eighty-five Soviet institutions. So I had much library business to conduct. In particular, I was making final plans for a weeklong joint conference later in the fall in Moscow with the Lenin Library, the Soviet equivalent of the Library of Congress, on the role of a national library in building a democratic culture.

The father of the Library of Congress, Thomas Jefferson, knew that democracy had to be knowledge-based. His own wide-ranging library became the nucleus of a new library founded for the Congress in the new capital of Washington at the beginning of the nineteenth century. Delegations from the increasingly important parliamentary bodies of the Soviet Union in the late twentieth century had been fascinated with this linkage and were exploring with us the possibility of replicating in some modest form the support role that the Library of Congress's Congressional Research Service had come to provide for American legislators.

Whereas libraries attract little attention in the American media, Russian newspapers and television paid great attention to the rise of an independent library association in Moscow (a characteristic example of the new civil society emerging in Russia) and to the plight of deteriorating, neglected, and mismanaged libraries in the USSR generally. Seeking alternative models, the Russian media devoted special attention to the Library of Congress and had overwhelmed me on recent trips with requests to speak with librarians and to give interviews for newspapers, radio, and television.

I arrived in Moscow a week before the putsch, prepared for discussions with librarians who were increasingly insistent on freer access to knowledge, yet still largely subordinated to hard-line Communist officials dedicated to monopolizing knowledge and limiting access. The library conference thus facilitated a running dialogue with people on both sides of the barricades—but within a profession inherently sympathetic to freedom and at a place, the relatively modern Mezhdunarodnaia (International) Hotel, that was a few hundred yards from the center of the confrontation at the Russian White House.

The concurrently unfolding Congress of Compatriots took place in the mammoth Rossiia Hotel near Red Square and immersed me in an all-Russian group whose program of seminars was focused on precisely the subject of my own current research as a cultural historian: the search for a post-totalitarian Russian identity.

I had begun pursuing this question particularly in the provincial interior of Russia with lengthy trips in the summer of 1987 and the summer of 1990. I had given a lecture in Russian before a large invited audience at the residence of the U.S. Ambassador in late May 1991 on the subject "Russia in Search of Itself." Now I was invited in the special capacity of "honored guest" to the Congress of Compatriots to participate in and to chair various roundtables on aspects of that same problem. This congress also continued uninterruptedly throughout the crisis and brought me into direct and often deep dialogue with many from the Russian provinces as they became active in resisting the coup.

This book is my attempt to account for the sudden rout of the coup attempt and of the old politics of fear—and to explain the unexpected breakthrough to hope among the hitherto passive Russian people.

I did not try then as an eyewitness—and am not attempting now as a historian—to provide a definitive chronology of events or assessment of individual roles, let alone motives.[2] I draw on my involvement during that time with people at the two congresses, as well as with some of the officials, intellectuals, and ordinary people of Moscow that I had been dealing with since my first visit there in 1958. But this is, in the last analysis, only the very personal story of how one historian-observer saw the long fever of totalitarianism finally break in Moscow—and saw a transformation, perhaps even a transfiguration, begin in Russia.

2

An Ordinary Week in Moscow: August 12–18

Moscow during the week before the coup looked and felt very much as it had on most of my recent visits. I was met at the airport on August 12 by Mikhail Levner, the head of the Library of Congress's Moscow office, and by Ekaterina Genieva, the deputy head of the All-Union Library of Foreign Literature. They ensconced me in a suite at the cavernous Rossiia Hotel, and I started off on the usual round of calls that a Librarian of Congress was expected to make in Moscow.

The Russians have a certain fascination with the very idea of a library that collects almost everything, yet is totally accessible. I had come early to discuss a wide variety of projects that their central institutions wanted to undertake with the Library of Congress: the exchange of electronic bibliographical records with their Book Chamber, help for developing a miniature Congressional Research Service for their Supreme Soviet, and the possibility of adding to their national library system some new cultural institution in honor of Gorbachev.

I had been receiving inquiries from high-ranking Soviet officials about a proposed Presidential Library ever since Raisa Gorbachev visited the Library of Congress during the June 1990 summit. I discussed the idea with Deputy Foreign Minister Vladimir Petrovsky shortly after my arrival, and he agreed to join me in a meeting the following week with Valery Boldin, Gorbachev's chief of staff, who had been trying to enlist my involvement in an even more grandiose monument for Gorbachev: an "Institute of the Book" to be located inside the Kremlin.

Actually, lavish new projects seemed to me especially out of place in a country where existing libraries were in notorious disarray. I found everyone's solicitude over memorializing a still living leader a sign that some of the old patterns had not changed. At the same time, the unusual cordiality of a succession of Soviet officials I met with that week at the Ministries of Foreign Affairs and of Culture gave me the odd feeling that they saw a closer official association with America somehow as a means of enhancing their own legitimacy.

My meetings that week with professional rather than political people indicated a more practical interest in America—a desire to learn how American political and economic institutions actually work and might be relevant for Russia. The professionals, who were younger than the officials, were excited about the election in June of Boris Yeltsin as Russia's first democratic President and about the new possibilities they saw opening up through a more collaborative relationship with the West. I was astonished at the range and sophistication of the questions about the Library of Congress and other American institutions asked by listeners from all over Russia when I appeared, together with Levner, on the popular call-in radio show on the leading station of the reform movement, Echo Moscow, in the evening of Sunday, August 18.

But there was an underlying sense of uncertainty tinged with fear. Earlier that same evening (during the official kickoff dinner for the library conference at the Prague Restaurant), a high-ranking officer of the Book Chamber came over to my table and solemnly told me that there would soon be a return to dictatorship in Russia, but that it would last only a year.

That same official had criticized the guardedly optimistic lecture I had given in Moscow late in May entitled "Russia in Search of Itself." In that talk, before several hundred Russians who had been invited by Ambassador Jack Matlock to his residence at Spaso House, I saw Russia struggling between two ways of defining its post-totalitarian identity: an authoritarian nationalism that glorifies the state and the army, exercising discipline from the top down, and a new democracy that seeks to build participatory and accountable economic and political institutions from the bottom up.

I had expressed my belief that Russia now had a chance to overcome the classic split between its Slavophile and Westernizing impulses and to create a new Russian identity that looked outward to liberal Western institutions yet also inward to conservative cultural values. Everything depended on whether the coming catharsis would be a nationalistic one based on purges, external enemies, and internal scapegoats or a deeper, moral catharsis within individuals involving the rebirth of conscience and the transcending of violence.

Believing that this analysis provided encouragement and perspective for the democratic movement, Konstantin Lubenchenko, the leader of a 190-member group of reformist deputies in the Supreme Soviet, arranged for its publication in the leading Moscow journal, *Independent*

Gazette. Its appearance during the unprecedented Russian presidential election campaign prompted an unprecedented official protest by the Soviet Embassy in Washington, apparently at the behest of some of the people behind the putsch.[3]

I was invited to repeat the lecture on the Thursday before the putsch at Moscow's leading center of progressive humanistic dialogue, the Library of Foreign Literature. In the rich discussion that followed, I sensed an enthusiasm for the ideal of democracy rerooted in religion that had not been so noticeable when I had spoken in May. But some of the young priests present seemed worried. The brilliant linguist who heads the library, Viacheslav Ivanov, noted that there had not yet been any action taken on his year-old official request as a People's Deputy of the all-union parliament for an investigation into the mysterious axe murder in September 1990 of the spiritual leader of democratic Christianity in Russia, Father Aleksandr Men.

The sense of unresolved, overhanging problems deepened at the reception Ivanov hosted after my talk at his dacha in Peredelkino. Ivanov's gifted Georgian collaborator and fellow Deputy, Tomas Gamkralidze, described the descent into the maelstrom that the democratically elected leader of Georgia, Zviad Gamsakhurdia, was imposing on his small country. One of the guests turned to me and noted wearily: "Unfortunately, democracy seems to lead us into chaos rather than out of it."

My two most constant companions during that first week, Katya Genieva and Misha Levner, punctuated their generally cheerful and invariably professional conversation with occasional observations about rising reactionary forces, which heightened the sense of foreboding.

Katya Genieva is the very embodiment of the type of strong women who have done so much to keep Russian tradition alive throughout the Soviet period. She reminded me of the widow of the great poet Osip Mandelshtam, Nadezhda, in whose kitchen I had first met twenty-five years ago the same Viacheslav Ivanov she now served as deputy. Like Nadezhda Mandelshtam, Katya loved English literature and was a devout Orthodox believer. She and Ivanov had been called in to direct the Library of Foreign Literature as a result of a lengthy strike against Communist control, but she now seemed pessimistic about the possibilities for any more such democratic revolts from below. The party apparatus, she observed, was determined to let things go no further and had sought to isolate the democratic infection by excluding their library from the local committee arranging the international library conference. All of my lectures and roundtables in Moscow were held at their library during this trip—mostly under the auspices of the Congress of Compatriots organized by Yeltsin's Russian government rather than the sponsorship of the library conference organized by the central Soviet Ministry of Culture.

Misha Levner had quietly been accumulating for the Library of Congress a magnificent collection of the new independent publications that were springing up under glasnost like mushrooms after the rain. From a small office in the Soviet Academy of Sciences' Library of Natural Sciences, he ran our Moscow office and accompanied me on my visits to libraries and bookstores. Rarely one to speak of personal matters, he nevertheless once mentioned that he had been insulted and threatened by an anti-Semitic gang in a subway station shortly before my arrival. He saw it as an isolated act of hooliganism, but it seemed to me to echo an attitude that I had found in a growing number of the new independent journals that Levner had collected for the Library of Congress.

Turning one nationality against another and everyone against the Jews had long been a tactic of Russian reactionaries for imperial crisis management; this kind of negative nationalism seemed to be gathering new strength by attacking old scapegoats. A large cartoon in one of the new papers, labeled *Peres-troika*, showed former Israeli prime minister Shimon Peres controlling both Gorbachev and Yeltsin with marionette strings.

I have become sufficiently Russified over the years to feel the need for respite in the countryside after too much discourse with Moscow officials and intellectuals. I had resolved to use this preparatory week to make my first ever visit to the rustic rural retreat of the great writer with whom my life as a student of Russian culture had begun: Leo Tolstoy. I had first read *War and Peace* as a boy during World War II, when a White Russian lady had told me that this book explained why Russia was able to hold out at the Battle of Stalingrad. I later came to feel that the "peace" part of the title had something to do with the restorative power of the Russian countryside. I was driven off to Tolstoy's estate at Yasnaya Polyana, for an unforgettable day with no other tourists around, by a young scholar from the Gorky Institute of World Literature, Anatoly Petrik, and by V. Ya. Lazarev, the editor of the new magazine of Russian culture, *Our Heritage.*

They allowed me to be alone with my thoughts in the open space that lies between the high grass and the high branches of the towering trees that one finds south of Moscow. This is a special kind of ambient space: private, yet suitable for expansive meditation; speckled with sunlight, yet roofed and carpeted. It is a rustic, yet domesticated outdoors, unlike either the closed forest to the north or the open steppe farther south.

Each of the four rooms in which Tolstoy wrote different parts of *War and Peace* and *Anna Karenina* had a window with its own distinctive and variegated treescape. My thoughts went back to Tolstoy's story "Three Deaths," in which a tree dies more nobly than man or beast, as I walked along paths the writer himself had once taken—all the way to the distant spot under the "green stick" where he played as a boy and where he was finally laid to rest.

It was a beautiful summer day. On the way back we stopped off for a home-cooked meal with Lazarev's relatives in the city of Tula. I returned to Moscow with a warm feeling about things that endure and was encouraged that the ordinary people who sold us apples by the road were as concerned as Moscow intellectuals about the degradation of the environment. They referred to a local chemical plant that had polluted the local water supply as "our little Chernobyl."

Back in Moscow, nothing seemed out of the ordinary. I spent Friday, August 16, at the annual meeting of the heads of national libraries, which was held at the Ministry of Culture building on the Arbat rather than in a library, as if to remind us that the central bureaucracy was still in charge. Visiting the exhibition hall for the international library congress, I noted that the Lenin Library displayed only a massive, utopian model for a future national library building and not one item from the present crumbling facility. It reminded me of the first architectural models I ever saw from the Soviet Union: the megalomaniacal depictions of future projects shown at the 1939 World's Fair in New York at a time when the gulag empire was at its height. Not much has changed, I thought, in the Soviet penchant for masking present failures with future promise.

A sunny, relaxing Sunday left me feeling mellow about the Russians' capacity to muddle through in spite of their system. I stayed over the weekend at the residence of the extremely able Chargé d'Affaires of the American Embassy, Jim Collins, together with our excellent acting Deputy Librarian of Congress, Winston Tabb. The three of us set off with Levner for the open-air flea market at Izmailovo. I then went to the Mezhdunarodnaia Hotel for some preliminary meetings of the library congress, then on to a reception for librarians hosted by a new entrepreneurial cooperative from the Russian information industry, and finally to talk with Russia by radio from the cramped, two-room studio of Echo Moscow.

Back at the Rossiia Hotel, the lobby was in the usual preconference turmoil as large numbers and various types of Russian emigrés and provincial Russians began arriving for the Congress of Compatriots and asking the harassed organizing committee all kinds of questions about the bewildering variety of trips and roundtables listed on the program. I retreated with Levner to my suite, reviewed with him my own crowded schedule for the week ahead, and drifted off to sleep expecting nothing much better or worse than I had experienced in dozens of previous trips since I first visited the USSR in 1958.

I was awakened earlier than expected the next morning by Misha Levner, who called me about 7 A.M. on Monday, August 19, with the news that something called the State Committee on the Extraordinary Situation had proclaimed Gorbachev ill and had taken over the government. From that moment forward, my life went into a kind of overdrive. For three days and nights I slept very little and lived largely on a portable supply of granola bars as I tried to keep up both with my original schedule of obligations and with the historical drama that I knew was unfolding around me. I circulated almost constantly between places of open-air confrontation and debate (Manezh Square and Gorky Street near the Kremlin and the space around the Yeltsin White House) and indoor official places where supporters and opponents of the coup attempt were often uneasily present at the same meetings. It was, for me, a dizzying, often surrealistic experience, but I gradually sensed that there was, for Russia, some method in the madness, some direction to the disarray.

It rapidly became clear after Misha's call that a political putsch was under way. Television and radio carried only bulletins from the junta, along with diversionary classical music and ballet. Long lines of tanks were moving into the center of Moscow by the time I set off with the Compatriot group to attend its opening service: a morning Liturgy for the Feast of the Transfiguration in the Kremlin's Cathedral of the Assumption at 10 A.M.

Opposition was already evident from the thinly veiled anger of many of the leaders of the Congress of Compatriots as they gathered at 9:30 A.M. in the north lobby of the Rossiia Hotel before going to the church service. No one believed the story about Gorbachev's illness, and many of the host committee who were also delegates to the Russian parliament seemed to be heading out for some destination other than the cathedral.

Many others seemed too frightened to speak; those who did had no prescriptions. But everyone in the lobby seemed to agree on the diagnosis: the Communist power elite had launched a coup d'état designed to turn back the tide of reform. In the process of trying to revalidate the politics of fear, the Extraordinary Situation Committee created an unprecedented political confrontation in Moscow on the first day of the putsch: August 19, 1991.

PART TWO

Fever Break

3

The Crisis of Coercion: August 19

Reduced to its essence, political power is based on both moral authority and physical force. One group of people cannot tell another group what to do without having both recognized norms for legitimacy and recognizable means of enforcement. Twentieth-century totalitarianism added something new to both sides of this classical formula.

Political authority had previously rested mainly on either transcendent authority conferred by religious coronation or on constitutional authority conferred by popular election. German Nazism and Soviet Communism based their authority on a new kind of secular ideology that promised to accomplish human perfection by conferring unlimited authority on a political organization dedicated to spreading and deepening that ideology.

Physical force had previously been exercised mainly by the limited military organs of a dynastic or national state, which enlisted engineering talent to defend its external borders and to maximize its internal tranquility. The new totalitarian states, however, sought to advance a universal end with infinitely varied means of coercion. They saw their ideologies as scientific truths destined to obliterate both human variety and traditional boundaries. Everyone everywhere was a potential recruit in the scientifically sanctioned cause, which manifested and sustained itself in the applied science of weaponry: the mass mobilization of people no less than the mass production of missiles.

The ultimate weapon in the totalitarian armory had been the controlling, coercive force of the Communist Party of the Soviet Union. It is easy to forget in the aftermath of its demise that this was, quite simply, the most powerful, most long-lived, and most effective political machine of the twentieth century, measured by the raw, physical criteria of its ability to perpetuate itself in power, dispense patronage, and atomize or eliminate opposition.

The Leninist political machine, which was created in 1903 and seized power in St. Petersburg in 1917, became the core of a formally organized worldwide movement until the Comintern was abolished during World War II. The machine became even more important after the war, which relegitimized the Soviet Union as a nation and extended its power over Eastern Europe. Having purged itself under Stalin of its international connections and its idealistic originators, the Leninist machine was free to focus its undivided attention on extending and deepening the imperial power of the Soviet state.

Stalin's heirs and beneficiaries were relatively uniform apparatchiks: trained as engineers, apprenticed as local organizers, and tested for leadership by a hierarchical ladder that eliminated individual thought and required ritual participation in the periodic purges of both "left" and "right" deviations.

Khrushchev and Brezhnev were profoundly vulgar men, devoid of either the aristocratic and religious culture of nineteenth-century Russia or the cosmopolitan and urban culture of early-twentieth-century Russia. But there was a certain animal brilliance in the way each of these Leninist leaders denounced his predecessor, divided his rivals at home, anesthetized opponents abroad, and, above all, controlled the public agenda. Over the thirty-eight years in which these two protégés of Stalin led the USSR, every American President entered during his first term into a legitimizing summit conference with the head of the Leninist machine, who succeeded in focusing the discussion mainly on the one subject in which the Leninists were genuinely competitive with the West: weapons of mass destruction.

The domestic equivalent of weapons of mass destruction was the technology of mass control, which continued to function even as the legitimacy of Communist ideology withered away. The Leninist machine increasingly relied on physical force and psychological fear. Real control devolved onto the inner apparatus or *nomenklatura.* The last two of Stalin's geriatric heirs, Yury Andropov and Konstantin Chernenko, were veterans respectively of the cruelest of internal security forces: the KGB and the Ministry of Internal Affairs border guards.

Gorbachev is a pure child of this party elite, the Russian equivalent of a chief lifeguard in Palm Springs. He was presiding over the resort area of Stavropol, where the overweight, geriatric leadership came to take the waters at the spa. They brought Gorbachev back to Moscow to preside over the oligarchy's long-delayed transition to a postwar, post-Stalinist generation of party leadership. Once in power, Gorbachev initially inclined toward authoritarian methods, calling for greater work discipline, opposing alcohol, and consolidating ministries into ever more gigantic conglomerates.

When I asked Gorbachev at a state dinner in December 1987 what word he would like written on his epitaph to describe what he had done for his country, he replied *di-namichnost:* dynamism. To generate dynamism in a stagnant society, he launched unusually radical reforms, but in the manner of a Leninist: playing off against each other left and right oppositions, while continuously consolidating his own power by invoking a vague policy slogan (*perestroika*) that only he could define. After creating new parliamentary institutions, which brought younger professional people into the political process as a liberal counterweight to the conservative party bureaucracy, Gorbachev built himself a super-presidency beyond the control of either. But as his authority weakened, he turned sharply to the right in the fall of 1990, then partway back to the left in late April 1991, when he agreed that a new union treaty should cede some real power back to the republics. Having gained more formal power than any Soviet leader since Stalin, Gorbachev may have had by the summer of 1991 even less authority within the USSR than the miserable Chernenko, whom he had succeeded.

Authority, however, was being reconstituted by the democratic opposition that was welling up from below and in from the periphery of the USSR. In almost every parliamentary election in which there was a genuine contest in 1990, democratic forces prevailed over reactionary ones; in June 1991, Boris Yeltsin was directly elected President of the Russian Republic—the first popularly legitimized ruler in Russian history.

Yeltsin and the newly elected democratic leaders of such large cities as Moscow, Leningrad, and Sverdlovsk had authority without real power. The Leninist machine had power without authority. Meanwhile, power was becoming its own authority, as the three armed forces—the Army, the KGB, and the Internal Affairs police—used violence against the restive non-Slavic peoples of the USSR in Georgia, Azerbaijan, Armenia, and Lithuania.

The moral authority of the Gorbachev government disintegrated amid its failure to acknowledge awareness of, let alone accept responsibility or make amends for, the bloodletting by armed Russians in Georgia and Lithuania. The Russian military intervention to stop interethnic fighting between Armenians and Azerbaijanis in Baku in January 1990 had produced an ominous mothers' revolt in Russia itself against deploying draftees in domestic warfare. The power in the central military–political machine that held the empire together coalesced in the attempt of the putsch to reassert authoritarian central control on August 19 in order to prevent the new union treaty from being signed into law on the following day.

What had been a struggle for legitimacy all over the union between the Leninist machine and a diffuse democratic movement suddenly became a focused struggle for power in Moscow. The so-called State Committee on the Extraordinary Situation in the USSR was an eight-man junta that included every governmental authority needed for political–military mobilization—the leaders of the Internal Affairs and Defense Ministries and the KGB, the effective heads of both industry and agriculture, and the Vice President and the Prime Minister of Gorbachev's government. No one in Gorbachev's cabinet except the Minister for Environment (the lone academic, Nikolai Vorontsov) denounced the putsch; Gorbachev's own chief of staff, Valery Boldin, helped craft it. Everything that had historically functioned from the top down in the entire Soviet period was on the side of the coup.

The junta's basic documents did not even speak about socialism or Communism. Its original "Address to the Soviet People" appealed to "compatriots" and "citizens" rather than "comrades" to rise up and defend the "motherland" rather than the Soviet Union. An almost apocalyptic accumulation of woes—cynicism, egoism, chaos, lawlessness—could be dispelled only if "everyone shows patriotic readiness" to contribute to "the rebirth of our fatherland."[4] At its press conference, the junta stressed its legality and its intention to continue the process of reform once the six months of dealing with the "extraordinary situation" had passed.[5]

The junta's preoccupation at its secret preparatory gathering on Sunday, August 18, was with the man at the top, Gorbachev, who had allowed himself to be isolated in a vacation spot in the Crimea (as Khrushchev had been when he was ousted from power twenty-seven years earlier). The group that went to see Gorbachev late that Sunday afternoon hoped Gorbachev himself would sign on with the putsch. His vacillation and indecisiveness had long encouraged the people around him to confront him with *faits accomplis* rather than argumentation if they wanted to get something done. The junta was dominated politically by people Gorbachev himself had appointed. Gorbachev had frequently discussed with them the idea of assuming extraordinary powers, and he had collaborated with them in instructing local party organizations to make preparations for a possible exercise of emergency powers. Gorbachev's closest personal friend, the head of the Supreme Soviet, Anatoly Lukianov, claimed that the proclamation of special powers to deal with the "extraordinary situation" in the USSR was to come the day after the signing of the Union Treaty. But the military participants in the coup clearly wanted to prevent the treaty from coming into being—and they dominated the Sunday afternoon confrontation with Gorbachev after militarily sealing him and his entourage off from outside contact.[6]

This sudden intrusion of the higher military command into politics was without precedent in Russian history but was amply foreshadowed during the previous year by increasingly strident criticisms of democratization and decentralization by the Minister of Defense, Dmitry Yazov, and by Gorbachev's former chief military adviser, Marshal Sergei Akhromeev. The top military command had been forced to endure a retreat without victory from Afghanistan; a political withdrawal from Eastern Europe; the humiliation of a favored former client, Saddam Hussein; and now the accelerating disintegration of the traditional Russian empire itself. They had already made common cause with the paramilitary power of the KGB and the Ministry of Internal Affairs in supporting earlier attempts in the Russian parliament to depose Yeltsin during March 1991, and in the all-union parliament to transfer executive power from Gorbachev to Prime Minister Valentin Pavlov in June 1991.

On August 5, the day after Gorbachev had left for his Crimean vacation, Yazov and key military leaders met with KGB leaders and ordered a staff study of the possibilities and problems of declaring a state of emergency in the country.[7] Though the study reached the conclusion that public opinion would not support such a move, Vladimir Kriuchkov nevertheless ordered the staff on August 14 to draw up detailed plans for establishing a temporary emergency regime in the USSR. Setting up headquarters in the village of Mashkino, the staff drew up the first draft of documents later used by the junta, which first assembled fully with the clear purpose of seizing power in the afternoon of Saturday, August 17.

With the military and KGB now joined with Pavlov and Gorbachev's other key political appointees, the first task was to force the indecisive President either to endorse the new emergency regime or to resign in favor of Vice President Yanaev—or else to neutralize him until the new junta was securely in power.

The Deputy Minister of Defense, Valentin Varennikov, and the Deputy Chairman of the Defense Council, Oleg Baklanov, made the pitch to Gorbachev. Whether he astutely sensed their ineptitude or genuinely rebelled at their treachery, Gorbachev refused either to sign on with the putsch or to sign off on his presidency. The attempt to legalize matters in a dacha discussion was over, and the way was open for a direct military move in Moscow.

The chosen tactic was a massive *show* of force without any *use* of force in the capital city in support of the eight-man State Committee on the Extraordinary Situation in the USSR, which was announced at daybreak on Monday the 19th. By 7:00 A.M. an immense military force was taking up positions in and around Moscow. Intimidation seemed to be working all throughout that first day. Television and radio came under the control of the putsch, as tanks and armored personnel carriers surrounded key places of communication and assembly. Most of Moscow simply went about its business in apathy and resignation. There were only a few small demonstrations and no response at all to the only concrete call for opposition: the appeal of the RS-FSR (Russian Republic) government for a general strike.

I found more resignation than resistance to the putsch at the opening ceremonies on the nineteenth of both of the congresses I was there to attend. When the service for the Compatriots in the Cathedral of the Assumption concluded, the Patriarch had taken no apparent note of the tanks that could be heard rumbling into nearby Red Square. The Soviet Minister of Culture, Nikolai Gubenko, seemed to be protecting both his flanks at the opening of the library conference; he said that there was indeed an extraordinary situation in the country, which, however, should not prevent the conference from continuing or him from eventually bringing greetings from Gorbachev.

Aleksandr Zakharov, the director of the Library of Natural Sciences of the Soviet Academy of Sciences, did not conceal his approval of the return to order and discipline that the junta promised. He had taken down his picture of Gorbachev and replaced it with a picture of flowers (the equivalent in decor of replacing real news programs with classical ballet on television during the crisis); he also had broken out a celebratory bottle as he watched the junta's announcements on television while waiting for me and my colleagues from the Library of Congress to visit his library (in which our Moscow office is housed). He was in an expansive mood at the reception he hosted for us in the early afternoon, speaking more about his own military background (as a former commander at the top secret space center of Baikonur) than about libraries.

Walking back from the library meetings in the midafternoon to the command center of the Congress of Compatriots at my hotel, I could observe little of the fraternization that later developed between the young tank drivers and ordinary citizens. People, it seemed, were trying not to notice the armored invasion, though a few women were crowding in on two tanks that had become isolated from the others on Gorky Street and were accusing the drivers of "attacking your own mothers."

At the late afternoon press conference hastily summoned by the conveners of the Congress of Compatriots, a shadowy functionary whom I had seen in the background before at Soviet official gatherings attempted to instill caution if not fear into the returning emigrés by pointing out that the conference was a creation of the Yeltsin government—implicitly suggesting that the visitors distance themselves from Yeltsin's resistance to the new central government. Toward the end of the conference, news arrived that the junta had itself held a press conference and had represented some initial comments of Bush and Mitterand as proof of international willingness to accept the change so long as existing international treaties were respected.

Coming out of this discouraging meeting as dusk settled in, I wended my way partly on foot, partly by bus through the largely indifferent and preoccupied crowds to the

Tchaikovsky Concert Hall on the broad Garden Ring Street, where the formal opening of the Congress of Compatriots was to take place. Most of my brief conversations en route seemed to suggest that political shrewdness as well as military might was on the side of the putsch. One small trickle of rather unkempt young people was chanting *Yel-tsin! Yel-tsin!* and heading toward the White House, but they were engulfed by a mob of people pushing half toward a bus, half toward a food vendor. I remembered Pasternak's image of a Moscow crowd pushing onto the subway as suggesting the mass society on its way to self-destruction: "Posterity shoved on to perils."[8]

I thought how skillfully the putsch had preempted the issue of Gorbachev's unpopularity and the popular fears that privatizing reforms would only make things worse. Just five days before the coup, a party-commissioned public opinion poll had been published, showing that 79 percent of Russians favored continued state control over most industrial enterprises.[9] Talking with a pair of minor officials sympathetic to the coup before the ceremony started in the Concert Hall, I realized how simple it all seemed to Leninist professionals: The great mass of the people is indifferent, the democratic opposition is amateurish and divisible, and—above all—everyone is basically afraid not just of the Leninist machine but of breaking away from the cocoon of order and predictability it had historically provided.

When one of these self-confident apparatchiks pointed out to me that "even Gorbachev's closest associate, Boldin, supports the new committee," I realized that my scheduled meeting with Boldin would not take place. I thought how bizarre it would have been to talk with Boldin about a cultural monument to the man with whom he had worked so closely yet must have been secretly working against.[10] I recalled my own disturbing talk with Boldin early in June 1991, during Yeltsin's presidential campaign. Boldin had attacked Yeltsin and the democratic movement in the distinctive way that Leninists combine lofty contempt for someone else's "childishness" with flattering expressions of certainty that I "as a student of Russian history" would concur with his more "realistic" view.

In the presence of a half-dozen other Gorbachev courtiers who sat silently in on that June meeting, Boldin had suggested that the attempt of the Russian federation to juxtapose its laws to those of the Communist Party and the all-union power structures was simply "playing at politics" (*politikanstvo*). For this apparatchik-in-chief, the entire business of electoral campaigns and parliamentary deliberations was itself the main cause of the "extraordinary situation" in the USSR, a disorder that could be dispelled only by reasserting central authority.

Boldin appears to have been a key figure in Gorbachev's reactionary turn late in 1990, playing up to Gorbachev's vanity by insisting that he alone could save the USSR from disintegration, feeding him KGB tapes of Yeltsin's conversation from Boldin's bulging safe, and looting the vast files of the "general section" of the archives of the Central Committee (which Boldin had controlled for ten years) to build a Presidential Archive for Gorbachev in the Kremlin. But, like a true Bolshevik, Boldin was ready to betray an individual in order to perpetuate the system. He had evidently been working for the putsch for some time before joining the group that confronted, in the Crimea on August 18, the man with whom he had worked intimately for fifteen years.

Three elements came into play in the afternoon of August 19 and began to provide an unexpected, original counterweight to the hitherto seemingly overwhelming power of the junta. There was the image of a leader, a circle of supporters, and the dispatch of messengers.

First and most important was the unforgettable image of Boris Yeltsin climbing onto a tank at midday and defying

the junta before a small group of supporters outside the
White House. Ivan Silaev, the Prime Minister of Yeltsin's
Russian government, had already that morning announced
defiance of the anticonstitutional government coup at a
press conference inside the Russian government building.
But the appearance of the elected President himself had an
electrifying impact as it was played back into Moscow on
CNN and was talked about as people compared notes after
work.

The poet Yevgeny Yevtushenko was so inspired that he
wrote a poem about that moment that was both better and
shorter than any in recent memory:

> This August day will be glorified
> in songs and bows.
> Today we are a nation,
> no longer fools.
> It would be full.
> And Sakharov alive has come
> to save this—our parliament—
> lighting his glasses cracked by the ground.
> The conscience of
> —even in the tanks—
> Yeltsin rises on the turret
> and around him there are no ghosts
> of the past Kremlin rulers—
> but real Russians—not yet vanished,
> and are tired within them—
> victims of the lights—
> No, never again,
> Russia will be on its knees.
> With us are Pushkin, Tolstoy.
> With us are people forever awakened.
> And the Russian parliament
> like a wounded marble swan of freedom

defended by our people
swings into immortality.[11]

Yevtushenko and a string of others gravitated to the White
House and began delivering from the balcony speeches that
were more concise and more inspirational than any Russian
rhetoric in living memory. The confused populace of Moscow had already heard about or seen leaflets proclaiming
the nonrecognition of the putsch by the government of the
Russian Republic; most knew that its parliament had gone
into immediate and continuous session inside the White
House, providing an alternative legitimacy and a kind of
countergovernment. But the image of the President seemingly quieting a tank provided the simple icon everyone
needed to engage the emotions in a society where words
have often been debased and where words alone have never
been enough.

Here was a moving image—in every sense of the word.
Yeltsin seemed to be thrust up by the people atop the tank,
rendering it somehow insignificant, attracting others to his
side. It was a reprise on the iconic image from Tiananmen
Square of a lonely boy standing in front of a tank making it
change course. But Yeltsin was not alone on an unprotected
square in this icon. The massive White House was in the
background; around him was the youthful chorus of some
Russian opera yet to be composed or liturgy yet to be written. Yeltsin seemed to be its mature, bass-voiced hero or
priestly celebrant.

Out of nowhere, it seemed, came videotapes, crude pho-
tos, and xeroxed sketches of this moment. The feeling
spread that something far more than politics was involved in
what was going on—something that required the three-
colored flag of prerevolutionary Russia, icons of St. George
slaying the dragon, and a host of other celebratory, mythic
elements to spill out all over Moscow by sunset.

The face and hands were the only parts of a saint depicted as flesh in Russian icons—and left uncovered by the metal plates tacked onto them over time. The image of Yeltsin was of a smiling face and a raised—yet beckoning—fist. It was made all the more powerful by the contrast Russians subliminally made with Yeltsin's rival, the nominal leader of the putsch, Gennady Yanaev, whose frightened frown and trembling hands were all that people remembered from the televised press conference of the eight-man junta late in the afternoon of the nineteenth.

If the image of a brave alternative leader inside the White House provided the first and most important counterweight to the junta's aura of inevitability, a second counterweight was added by the human wall of supporters outside that had taken permanent shape by the early evening of the nineteenth. At the formal opening meeting of the Congress of Compatriots in the Tchaikovsky Concert Hall, I got some sense of why those people had showed up. Our largely apolitical Compatriots group was suddenly immersed in the broader society's crisis of conscience. A Russian emigré made a moving speech in opposition to the coup, and—amid cries of "provocation" from some present—invited those present to rise for a moment of solidarity with the missing Gorbachev and the embattled Yeltsin. Everyone was suddenly confronted with a small but highly public decision: whether or not to stand up. Many remained seated and gave hostile looks to the hundreds who stood up. Those who rose soon found themselves making another choice: to go themselves to the White House rather than stay on for the cultural program. Despite the darkness and the rain, the miscellaneous groups that left the meeting found a far larger and more heterogeneous crowd outside the White House than had been there during the day.

The crowd was beginning to take the shape of a circle

38

around the White House. Like waves rolling outward from a central point, an alternative allegiance seemed to be radiating to the broader society. From within the building, the inner circle guarding Yeltsin had already added a peripheral circle of defenders by the windows. Now a larger human ring was beginning to form outside.

The circle was drawn in from all over Moscow, as young people arrived from every direction with materials for surrounding the White House with barricades. Unconsciously, spontaneously, Moscow was replicating the defense of a parliament building by a wall of citizens that had occurred earlier that year in Vilnius, the embattled capital of Lithuania. Images of ordinary people encircling their elected government to defend it against armored military assault had been banned from Soviet television in January but were subsequently broadcast and emblazoned on youthful imaginations. Now, in Moscow itself, without any formal commands from anywhere, Russians were drawing their own circle in the sand.

Even more important than the circle of defenders was the third element in the mounting resistance to the coup: the dispatch of messengers. At 3 P.M. on August 19, General Konstantin Kobets, chairman of the Russian Republic's State Committee for Defense, summoned a meeting of Russian parliamentarians within the White House and enlisted them in an ambitious plan to go out in small teams to engage in aggressive dialogue with the armored troops that had entered Moscow and appeared to be menacing the White House.

Kobets himself went immediately on the offensive, telephoning military officers he knew to urge noncompliance with an illegal coup, as did Yeltsin's Vice President, a former air force hero in Afghanistan, Aleksandr Rutskoi. Meanwhile teams went forth in the late afternoon and early evening to tell soldiers all over Moscow about the putsch and to convince them that their orders came from illegal authority.

The pattern was to send a uniformed soldier loyal to the Russian government along with an elected deputy of the Russian parliament. They sought to persuade the soldiers that Yeltsin's cause was both militarily honorable and politically legal, in contrast to that of the junta.

One key team was formed by Lieutenant Colonel Sergei Yushenkov and a parliamentary deputy and head of the Russian Christian Democratic Movement, Viktor Aksiutich. They sought out the commanding officer of a tank battalion from the elite Tamansky Division stationed on a nearby embankment. They engaged this potential lead attacker, a Major Evdokhimov, in dialogue and persuaded him to talk with Rutskoi, who in turn convinced him to transfer the allegiance of his ten-tank unit to the Yeltsin government.[12] This defection early in the evening on August 19 broke the military monolith and seemed to validate the image of Yeltsin mastering the tanks.

I remember standing in the rain outside the White House when the loudspeaker made the thrilling announcement that the attacking tanks had crossed over to the defending side. A rhythmic chant of *mo-lod-tsy, mo-lod-tsy* (good guys, good guys) was the crowd's response to this, the first of many communiqués that "Radio White House" broadcast periodically to its outer wall of supporters. This first announcement of an unprecedented change of allegiance by a military unit inspired a feeling that power was being not merely transferred but relegitimized. The announcer stressed that each tank would add to its crew one elected deputy of the Russian parliament, suggesting that physical force was at last being brought under the control of popularly elected authority.

The dispatch of messengers from the White House also

encouraged less visible forms of insubordination that enabled the resistance to survive that first night when the defenders were still small in number and disorganized. Much the most important internal resistance by junior officers on the first day occurred—unbeknownst to any of us at the time—within the ranks of the most ruthless and best-equipped strike force in the USSR: the 200-man antiterrorist unit of the KGB known as Alpha.

When it became evident that force would have to be used, and not merely displayed, against the defiant Yeltsin forces, Vladimir Kriuchkov, the head of the KGB, appears to have ordered this unit to prepare an assault on the White House. At 5:30 in the afternoon of August 19, the KGB Major General Viktor Karpukhin, already a Hero of the Soviet Union for his work with Alpha, summoned the leaders of the unit and told them to prepare to storm the building.

In the retrospective account that Alpha members provided after the coup had failed, they asked who gave the orders and were told simply "the government." Not even Kriuchkov, it appears, wanted to leave his fingerprints on an order to kill. The troops then allegedly entered a long period of soul-searching and discussion before definitively deciding not to attack at 3:00 A.M. despite well-worked-out plans that they claimed would have succeeded in twenty to twenty-five minutes. [13] Yeltsin first expected an attack at 6:00 P.M. and believed that it was rescheduled several times as the KGB added other units to the proposed force before fixing on 3:00 A.M. [14] But a decision not to attack that night had apparently already been made by 10:30 P.M., when the Alpha units returned to their barracks. [15]

It is always difficult to sort out the balance between idealistic and material motives in judging how people make decisions of this kind. But in attempting to explain how a well-trained, battle-tested unit of professional killers decided not to perform their mission, it seems right to look to ignoble, even animal reasons for their refusal to fight. The simple fact seems to be that this elite brigade within the feared Seventh Directorate (for personal surveillance) of the KGB feared for their lives. They believed that they faced six tanks and fifteen armored personnel carriers outside the White House and five hundred well-armed people inside the building.[16] They knew that this assault would not be as casualty-free as those on which their fearsome reputation had been based: the assault on the palace of the Afghan President, whom they murdered at the beginning of that war in 1979, and the storming of the Lithuanian television tower on behalf of a shadowy earlier Committee for National Salvation on January 13, 1991.

Alpha members were bitter at the treatment of the family of their one fatality in Lithuania, Viktor Shatskikh; a number had resigned soon thereafter. Clearly this was going to be much bloodier, and with no promise of glory or even of good treatment from their superiors. (They remembered that the forces on the spot had been left to take the blame for the bloody repression in Tbilisi in April 1989, after a long series of investigations by the politicians.) The age of the Russian Rambos was over. The burden of fear had shifted from the populace at large to the KGB itself.

Those of us outside the White House in the early evening of the nineteenth never knew that an attack had been ordered, just as those inside apparently never learned that it had been called off. But most of the still motley crowd around the White House were preoccupied not with dangers but with their own festive sense of improvisation and even celebration.

There was a good deal of singing and drawing of graffiti mixed into the shared task of perfecting and strengthening the barricades. Sacred and profane symbols were intermixed. A sketch of Major Evdokhimov as St. George appeared on the wall alongside the outline of a huge penis labeled "Yanaev." It occurred to me as the evening wore on that I was in the midst not just of a mobilization but of a carnival. I was reminded of the kermesse scenes in Breughel paintings and wondered if I was seeing a posthumous vindication of the concept developed by the great, long-suppressed critic of the Soviet era, Mikhail Bakhtin: the carnival as a way out of tyranny to freedom.

Bakhtin described the carnival as a "second life" for oppressed people, enabling them to celebrate their "temporary liberation from the prevailing truth and from the established order." He was referring to the medieval past but dreaming about the Russian future when he suggested that "all were considered equal during carnival"; hierarchies broke down, and "people were, so to speak, reborn for new, purely human relations."[17] A Ukrainian philosopher had already likened the entire era of perestroika to a carnival that mocked tradition and replaced the "monologue" of totalitarianism with a cacophony of voices, creating a variety of new possibilities.[18]

I wondered that evening whether the happening by the White House was destined to be what a real-life medieval carnival had generally been—an interlude in oppression more than a prelude to freedom. Bakhtin wrote that the "life of the carnival square" produced a "joyful relativity of all structure and order," leading to the "mock crowning and subsequent decrowning of the carnival king."[19] Was Yeltsin just king for a day, destined to be remembered more for his blasphemy against authoritarian norms than for his affirmation of democratic ideals? Was I witnessing just a faint echo of the demonstrations of the 1960s in the West, a foredoomed interlude—like the tragically brief Decembrist uprising of 1825—in the long authoritarian history of Russia?

I felt mildly reassured as I walked back to my hotel late that night, because there seemed to be as many people coming to as going from the White House. I passed the metro station nearest the White House (appropriately named Barrikadnaia) and noticed that, though it was closed, people were still milling around and hauling off building materials from a nearby construction site to reinforce the barricades. The continuing flow of people helped account for the widely varying estimates of the actual crowd around the White House during the first day of the coup attempt. Comparing my own impressions with the notes and pictures of others, I would estimate that the numbers varied from about 30,000 in the late afternoon to about 10,000 when I left in the early morning.

I later learned, however, that the numbers subsequently fell even further, leaving the White House in effect without an outer wall of defenders altogether at a critical time on the second as well as the first night. This moment came just before dawn, when the metro reopened and most of the already reduced component went home for at least a brief respite.

The first twenty-four hours of the putsch were thus framed by two extraordinary moments of good fortune for the opposition: the failure of the junta to arrest Yeltsin in his dacha before he left for the White House at 6:00 A.M. on the nineteenth and the failure to storm the building when its outer defense was unmanned twenty-four hours later. As the dawn broke through the continuing drizzle on August 20, the second day of the coup, the outcome was unclear, but the fever of fear had broken.

~ 4 ~

The Mobilization of Hope: August 20

The second day of the coup pitted the new power of raw hope among ordinary people against the old reliance on raw power by the junta. Although the KGB had pulled back from an attack on the first night, the far larger units under the Ministers of Defense and Internal Affairs had not yet come into play. [20] The tactic of merely showing force had not paralyzed the opposition, but it was now all concentrated and localized in a single spot, where overwhelming military strength could physically ensure its total destruction. As one official put it to me early on August 20 in the brutal, clinical language that Leninists love: "We have brought the infection to a head. Now all we need to do is lance the boil."

But who would be the lancer? Whereas everyone defending the White House seemed willing to face death without thinking much about it, everyone in the junta was investing a flood of verbiage in the effort to get somebody else to face it for them. No one wanted the responsibility for launching a frontal attack during the day, now that all the world was watching. General Yazov spent much of the morning trying to get the Air Force to agree to attack the White House from above, but its commander, General Yevgeny Shaposhnikov, refused—and later threatened to bomb the Kremlin if Yazov assaulted the White House. The KGB played with the idea of attacking from below, using twenty-four subterranean entry points, which were not known to the occupants of the White House themselves. (The Yeltsin forces could find only four of them even after a KGB officer had tipped them off.)

General Varennikov was the youngest and most militant member of the junta, but he had failed to recruit the most respected and ruthless of the younger military leaders, General Boris Gromov, in a conversation they had in the Crimea on August 18 just after his unsuccessful attempt to pressure Gorbachev into resigning or signing on. Gromov was Minister of Internal Affairs Boris Pugo's deputy and the key to enlisting that ministry's military forces, which were the best trained for urban combat. Gromov returned to Moscow from his vacation in the Crimean sanatorium on the night of August 19 and participated in military meetings with the junta but never fully joined the putsch.

I rose early on August 20 and was brought up to date on the rumors about what was happening over a quick breakfast with some Siberian participants in the Compatriots Congress. I realized how little my training as a historian had prepared me for the emotional experience of participating in the historic events of a country I had studied all my life. I was moved by the resistance to believe that it would somehow prevail, yet depressed by the thought that bloodshed seemed imminent and short-term repression almost unavoidable. I was, in short, as uncertain as anyone else about what would happen. But I was determined to stick to my scheduled obligations and decided simply to add on as many supplementary visits and conversations as I could physically endure in order better to understand the Russian people in this time of crisis. I began by taking a long walk across Red Square, up Gorky Street, along the Garden Ring, and back down the Arbat and Herzen Street to Manezh Square and the Kremlin.

The dominant impression I picked up on the streets that morning was not of imminent conflict but of the fuzzing of boundaries between the conflicting parties. Yeltsin supporters were actively talking with the soldiers, who seemed increasingly restless with their immobility and awkward in their prominent yet stationary positions. Both the crew-cut soldiers in the tanks and their ponytailed contemporaries from the barricades were being jostled by the familiar *dramatis personae* of the disintegrating economy: argumentative drunks, emotional old women telling everyone to go home, and foreign tourists taking pictures of each other and offering everyone cigarettes.

The carnival scene around the White House the night before seemed to be spreading to the streets—and, unbeknownst to us at the time, to the provinces.[21] But two new ingredients seemed to be present wherever people were clustering around tanks that morning in Moscow: the smell of flowers and the sound of women's voices.

Russians, like all Northern peoples, have a special fondness for flowers, and in late August they were blooming everywhere. As Muscovites went to work on the second day of the putsch and discovered the tanks still largely in the same places they had been the night before, they began bringing flowers to the young men inside. They seemed to be both expressing thanks that violence had been avoided and attempting to communicate friendship to the young people inside those formidable armored shells. When the soldiers inside the tanks refused to come out, Muscovites often simply left flowers on top of the tanks. When the soldiers did come out to talk, people often placed flowers in the barrels of their guns as a sign of appreciation and a signal, it seemed, for celebration.

It all seemed like a belated vindication in the East of the flower power that had been proclaimed by Western radicals during the 1960s. One could even hear at times the sound of rock music from that era playing on the tape recorders that were becoming part of the carnival.

But the dominant sound in the dialogue with the soldiers was that of women's voices. Women were taking the lead in trying to persuade the soldiers never to fire on their fellow Russians. Their intercession removed the conflict from the arena of one man's challenge to another. They were more persuasive than the disheveled young men from the barricades would have been in undercutting the only motivating argument that the junta had presented to the troops: that the people opposing them were nothing but young hooligans and spoiled students dodging the draft.

I left the carnival on the streets in the late morning for the corridors of the establishment to keep an appointment with the head of the publishing house of the Central Committee of the Communist Party. Like much of Moscow officialdom, he seemed far more concerned about the uncertainty of his own position than about the outcome of the crisis. He was one of those people who do not want historic events to be seen as such. He seemed anxious both to justify the formation of the Extraordinary Situation Committee and to reassure me that it would only stop the clock for a while, not turn it back. "There will be no fascism, I promise you," he said, escorting me out past a picture of Gorbachev that he still displayed, though not in a very prominent place.

I went next to the Library of Foreign Literature. There I talked with Viacheslav Ivanov, who had come directly from spending the night at the White House to brief his staff about the resistance. This was the way institutions all over

Moscow were kept informed, but the briefings at his library had special importance both because of the many meetings being held there for the two congresses and because the leading reformist journal, *The Independent Gazette*, had been given a home in Ivanov's library after it was proscribed by the junta.

By midafternoon, when I returned to the Hotel Rossiia, the spectacle of festive fraternization on the streets began to seem like a deceptive lull before the storm. Russians just back from the White House told me at the headquarters of the Congress of Compatriots that an attack was expected at 4:00 P.M. Many participants in the library conference were leaving Moscow, but my Library of Congress colleagues were staying on. I set off amid all the uncertainty at 3:45 to take part in three different events connected with the conference: a religious service in St. Basil's Cathedral, a reception in the Pushkin Art Museum, and the founding meeting, in a private flat, of a new Russian Bibliographical Society.

Russians in all three places revealed a welter of contradictory emotions. Reformers tended to be withdrawn, and high-ranking officials were nervously talkative. But there was a surprisingly large group that acted as if nothing were happening at all, or at least nothing that should interfere with establishing foreign contacts. Underlying everything was an unspoken sense that the carnival was over and something terrible was about to happen.

There was an eerie calm in a deserted Red Square as I made my way to a special church service for the library conference that began in St. Basil's Cathedral at 4:00, the very hour when the storming of the White House was expected.

St. Basil's Cathedral is more an exotic piece of sculpture than a place of worship. But inside the largest of the nine small chapels that make up its interior, a Bishop Viktor conducted a moving prayer service along with Father Boris Danilenko, the strong, soft-spoken librarian of the library within the Danilov Monastery in Moscow. I had worked with John Brademas, the dynamic President of New York University, who got the Onassis Foundation to set up a microfiche library in religious information for Father Boris's new establishment in 1988. It was somehow reassuring now to spend some quiet time paying prayerful homage to books and all they stand for in the presence of a man who was both a custodian of old values and a champion of new approaches.

At the end of the service I delivered a suggested text of an official statement of support for the democratic forces to the head of the International Federation of Library Associations, Hans-Peter Geh of Germany, who had also come to the service. I have never been fond of this kind of declamatory statement, which often seems designed more to make the speaker feel good than to do anything concrete for the people being spoken about. But many Russians had cited the urgent need for the West to speak up, and it was obvious that the freedom that libraries were just beginning to feel in the USSR would be completely reversed if the junta succeeded. I remembered the remark of my distinguished predecessor as Librarian of Congress, Archibald Macleish, that librarians were "the sentinels of freedom," so I thought some kind of sign should be given that the sentinels assembled in Moscow had not entirely gone to sleep on the watch. I framed a resolution of support for the democratization process as something favorable to libraries, and for the rapid release of President Gorbachev so that he could address our congress, as the Minister of Culture had suggested at the opening session. Mr. Geh and his staff expressed the traditional reluctance of international civil servants to have an international conference say anything that might in any way offend any of their hosts.[22]

50

I then went to a somewhat surreal official reception for the library conference held in the serenely neoclassical Pushkin Museum of Fine Arts. Soviet and foreign officials wandered with drinks through the elegant galleries, while some of the more democratic-minded Russian librarians took trays of food down to the museum guards, coat-check women, and others who were working overtime in the basement.

The setting sun briefly broke through the rain clouds and lit up the windows on the main staircase. This produced some haunting illumination for two spectacular exhibits of treasures from Eastern Christendom not previously altogether known to have been in the museum's possession: an early Coptic and a late Byzantine collection. I was reminded again of the cultural richness still to be discovered in the reserve collections of Russian museums and libraries. I imagined that those simple women I had earlier seen appealing to the soldiers were now praying for them before the omnipresent cheap reproductions of bad icons, while Soviet officials thinking only of themselves were parading here past these magnificent original icons, which they had long kept in hiding and were now barely even noticing.

Most people at the reception did not talk about the crisis and were simply—in T. S. Eliot's words—passing to and fro, talking of Michelangelo. But whenever I saw a small cluster, I knew they were discussing the faceoff that seemed headed for a showdown at the White House. The subject was so sensitive and the sense of danger so imminent that people talked about it only with trusted, like-minded colleagues. A reactionary cluster conferred in the impressionist gallery; a reformist group in front of painted Coptic textiles.

Those librarians who had visited the barricades before coming to the reception generally seemed more hopeful about what was happening than the Soviet officials, who kept darting out to make phone calls in search of the information they needed to keep their weather vanes adjusted.

I had a particularly chilling conversation on the way into the reception with a leading Communist Party official in the cultural world, S. G. Shuvalov. He was Vice Chairman both of the all-union Society, "the Book," and of another shadowy body that may have the longest name of all commissions in parliamentary history: The Commission of Nationalities of the Supreme Soviet of the USSR on Culture, Language, National, and International Traditions, and the Preservation of the Historical Heritage. Clearly things were not going very well in his commodious domain. He argued that a rapid and decisive consolidation of power by the junta was a matter of great urgency and that the very survival of a viable government and a coherent social structure was at stake. There was a tone of sincerity about his plea—along with an overtone of apocalyptic desperation.

I was relieved to escape early from this unreal gathering to a flat on the outskirts of Moscow, where some twenty-five scholars and librarians were celebrating the refounding of a humble but noble organization from prerevolutionary times: the Russian Bibliographical Society. I drove there with Misha Levner and Anatoly Petrik, the leader and dominant personality of the group, whom I had gotten to know on my trip to Yasnaya Polyana. He was the son of a Russian diplomat who had become an energetic entrepreneur in the burgeoning new information industry of Moscow. All those present at the flat were intellectuals of modest means like Irina Pozdeeva of Moscow University, an expert on the Russian Old Believers, and Gennady Popov, a pioneer in electronic bibliography at the all-union Book Chamber. They were dedicated professionals, and that evening they were creating yet another free institution for the rapidly developing civil society: the nongovernmental sector whose rising tide of publications Levner had been skillfully channeling into the Library of Congress collections. No officials were there except those they themselves were about to pick for this new private organization, to which they welcomed me and Christine Thomas from the British Library as honorary advisers.

Our hosts were about to bring in the main course of a dinner that had probably cost them each a week's salary when everyone suddenly fell silent before the television set, which up to then had been playing unnoticed in the background. The impassive woman who had been the media spokesperson for the junta suddenly came onto the screen and announced the proclamation of a total military curfew at 11:00 P.M. in the entire city of Moscow.

The Russian term *kommendantsky chas,* "the hour of the commandant," has a far more ominous ring than the English word curfew, which derives from *couvre feu*: covering the hearth fire before going to sleep. The announcement droned on with a long list of particulars, including a repetition of the junta's warrants for the arrest of Yeltsin and his advisers and a warning that special police would accompany the Moscow police (who were subordinate to the liberal Moscow government) to ensure enforcement.

The reaction among my quiet, essentially apolitical friends was impressive: total silence followed by one of the older women's quiet statement: "We must go now." No one said where, but the entire group rapidly cleared away the dishes and hurried down the crumbling concrete stairs of the apartment building into several crowded cars. The assumption was clear. I would go back to my hotel, and they would deal with whatever the night would bring. As Petrik's car threaded its way through secondary streets, the rain became heavier. I noticed new uniforms alongside the Moscow militiamen cordoning off new parts of the city.

When I was dropped off at the Hotel Rossiia, Anatoly said, with a mixture of offhand jauntiness and deep seriousness characteristic of many of the young participants in these events, "You must forgive us for having such a strange government." An older woman librarian quietly explained that they would all be going to the barricades. She said it was particularly important that Russians of her generation join the young, "since we are the ones who for so long remained silent."

It was a wrenching moment as we said our farewells, and they left in a car that I later learned was taking both Molotov cocktails and McDonald hamburgers to the White House. I did not know that night if I would ever see them—or indeed most of my Russian friends—again. In my hotel room, I tried to work on the lecture I was to give the next morning in the Library of Foreign Literature on the role of libraries in a democratic society. Instead, I kept thinking about these astonishing two days. I worried, too, about the director of that library, my friend Viacheslav Ivanov. I knew that both he and his son Leonid (the energetic compiler of a computerized database of joint venture opportunities for foreign investors) would surely be among those spending the night defending the White House.

There was a lot of praying done that night by people who had not had much practice at it. Patriarch Alexis II, head of the Russian Orthodox Church, addressed his own powerful prayer against bloodletting to potential assailants on the White House at 1:30 A.M., just before the final assault was expected. That prayer came too late to save three young men who had just been killed by armored personnel carriers and tanks near the intersection between the Garden Ring and Kalinin Prospect. But those were the only casualties of the night. They occurred a half-mile from the White House, and the tanks had in fact been moving in the opposite direction.

The White House, which had sent out SOS telephone calls and agitators to neutralize the army on August 19, turned into a magnet attracting people into its perimeter on

August 20. Small groups from all walks of life swelled the crowd around the building to more than twice the size of the previous day, reaching 70,000, perhaps even 100,000. In full expectation of an attack, Rutskoi and Kobets organized not just an effective defense but a mobilization of conscience.

At a crucial meeting inside the White House at 1:00 A.M., Yeltsin's Vice President, Rutskoi, and his closest associate, Gennady Burbulis, instructed the defenders to act as nonviolently as possible and to let everyone act as he wished in the event of the expected assault. They asked women to leave the building and the human wall to move 50 meters away to minimize casualties. Armed basically with nothing more than Kalashnikov automatic weapons and Molotov cocktails, they made the defense inside the White House an entirely voluntary undertaking, urging each person to examine his or her own conscience and often conflicting obligations to others to determine what role each should be prepared to play in the event of fighting. Not only weapons, but food and medical supplies flowed in during the second day. Each acquired its voluntary service and distribution center, as women set up canteen and first aid centers.

If ordinary people were flocking to the barricades and acquiring discipline, uniformed soldiers were staying away and resisting orders. A fresh division of elite troops moved in from Tula but remained outside the city, some of its soldiers having already joined the defenders of the White House after its commanding officer, Major General Aleksandr Lebed, talked personally with Yeltsin.[23] The commander of the Army's airborne forces, Colonel General Pavel Grachev, balked at launching a helicopter assault. General Shaposhnikov was in open opposition, threatening aerial countermeasures in the event of an assault. Defense Minister Yazov was unable to bring Shaposhnikov around in a face-to-face meeting in the late afternoon. Then, Ya-zov's tearful wife entered his office and implored him sim-ply to arrest all the civilian leaders of the putsch. His famous reply was that he could not be a traitor a second time; well into the next day he seemed anxious to preserve a shred of integrity by at least remaining loyal to his original sedition.

Throughout the night of the twentieth, the heads of De-fense, Internal Affairs, and the KGB were still solidly com-mitted to the putsch and in command of vast forces that were expected to storm the White House. The defenders did not use the Slavic word *groza*, which suggested a thunderstorm or the autocratic rages of Ivan the Terrible (*grozny*) to de-scribe what they feared. They used the professional military term *shturm*, taken from the German and used by Stalin to describe the military type of assault (*shturmovshchina*) he wanted made on the targets of his five-year plans.

The defenders were heartened by the belief that they were bringing laws to a country that had too long been ruled by forces operating beyond the law. The Russian parliament had been in virtually continuous session since midmorning of the nineteenth, basing everything the Yeltsin forces did on laws and sending out elected deputies to persuade the soldiers of the illegality of the coup. An effective executive branch was also functioning under Ivan Silaev, Chairman of the Russian Republic's Council of Ministers, who issued a steady stream of administrative decrees. All the military figures who joined the resistance stressed the legality of placing themselves under the elected officials and legislative authority of the Russian Republic, since the Soviet Union as a whole was now in the hands of those who had usurped authority from its President and did not even provide writ-ten orders for what they seemed to want done.

Many in the White House felt that Gorbachev as an unelected President lacked Yeltsin's legitimacy, but all ral-lied to the demand that he be restored to office in order to sustain the effort to build the rule of law. This was a recurrent theme of the best speeches delivered to the crowds outside the White House—those that inspired not only cheers, but tears. Elena Bonner, who had been one of Gorbachev's severest radical critics, brought forth one of the most thunderous ovations of the entire period with her concluding words:

Gorbachev is our president. We can judge him, but they cannot. They think they can direct and order us, feed us or not. . . . But we will show them, prove to them, that we are people, *people* and not just cattle [*bydlo*].[24]

Equally forceful were the words spoken to the defenders by Gorbachev's once and future Foreign Minister, Eduard Shevardnadze: "I am breaking the curfew together with you because we do not recognize their ukazes and we will not live by their laws." He demanded that the junta permit Gorbachev to appear in public, but added that "if he endorses the overthrow, we will ourselves judge him."[25]

Two bright young champions of the rule of law whom I had first met at the Library of Congress played a key role in the events of that day: Oleg Rumiantsev and Konstantin Lubenchenko. Rumiantsev, the head of Yeltsin's committee to draft a new constitution for the Russian Republic, rushed to the spot where the three young men were killed and helped calm the crowd to avoid further bloodshed.[26] Lubenchenko, who chaired an independent 190-person group of reform-minded legislators within the all-union legislature, helped block the attempts of Anatoly Lukianov to provide a patina of legislative legality for the putsch at the all-union level.[27] Lubenchenko got advanced warning for the Yeltsin forces of KGB plans for an assault. After the coup, he replaced the imprisoned Lukianov as Speaker of the all-union parliament.

It had not always been certain that the Russian Republic's Supreme Soviet would support armed resistance even to a usurping central government. Yeltsin had initially commanded only a slight majority of supporters in the legislature. His call for a general strike on the morning of August 19 was immediately denounced as an incitement to bloodshed by both the legislature's Vice Chairman, Boris Isaev, and the President of its Council of the Republic, Vladimir Isakov.[28] But the Yeltsin forces quickly overwhelmed those dissenting voices. The democratic deputies had grown in confidence after resisting the reactionary attempt to turn the parliament against Yeltsin in March. They themselves had marched in the front rank of the peaceful mass demonstrations in Moscow against the Leninist machine. Having formed a human wall of their own in March, they were prepared to help others organize an even more important one in August.

At 3:00 A.M. on August 21, Kriuchkov called the White House to tell Yeltsin there would be no assault that night. When dawn broke, many on the barricades again felt able to drift off on the early metros. I was encouraged not only by the good news brought back by friends from the barricades that the storm had not come but also by the way that message was conveyed on the still-controlled television. Even the junta's own announcer lingered over pictures of flowers on the tanks and the open fraternization of soldiers with the people during the preceding day on the streets of Moscow. He added only briefly at the end (in a sad voice and without showing any pictures) that three did perish during the night, implying that it was a tragic accident, an awful exception to the new atmosphere of hope in Moscow. Thus, by dawn of the second day, the hope for something different had penetrated even into the propaganda machine of the putsch.

When I reached the White House in the early morning

of August 21, it looked whiter than ever, largely because the weather was clearing. It is not a beautiful building, but it has a certain solid simplicity. The last lines of the poem Yevtushenko had written within it and recited from its balcony came back to me: "And the Russian parliament / like a wounded marble swan of freedom / defended by our people / swings into immortality."

A colorful small dirigible with a tricolor had been placed on top of the White House since the beginning, providing its only protection against air attack. It had been put there by one of the many private firms that rallied to the defense, a group called Ecosphere. It lifted my eyes up. As I looked around, I noticed that the White House seemed to form a center point for two surrounding rings of equally tall but quite different buildings. There was an outer ring of three identical Stalinist monstrosities: an apartment structure near the Barrikadnaia metro station, the Ministry of Foreign Affairs building near where the blood had been shed, and the Ukraine Hotel just across the river. There was also a closer, more nondescript group of newer buildings: the Mir Hotel; the headquarters of COMECON, the former East European common market (which some reactionaries sympathetic to the putsch called "the Torah" because it was shaped like an open book and thought to be a source of foreign "infection"); and the famous bug-laden, deserted building in the new compound of the American Embassy.

People now began to fear possible sniper fire aimed at Yeltsin from one of the hotels or the COMECON building more than a massive attack on his headquarters. No one could be sure, but the community of hope seemed to be winning, and—yes—the sun really was shining.

⧼ 5 ⧽

Russia in Search of Itself: August 21–24

The contest of power was over in Moscow, but Russia's search for a post-totalitarian identity had just begun. The first day had broken the back of fear. The second day had raised the face of hope. The next four days turned a transfer of power into the celebration of a people.

It was not immediately clear on August 21 that the putsch had failed, even after Yazov ordered the troops to withdraw early in the morning and a 3-mile column of armored forces began to leave Moscow. It was known by the early afternoon that there was a race on to get to the still incommunicado Gorbachev and that a plane carrying Yazov and Kriuchkov had taken off for the Crimea before Yeltsin's forces could stop them or send off their own plane carrying Rutskoi and Silaev. The crowd did not disperse around the White House, because people remembered how the tanks had retreated from Budapest in 1956 only to return with renewed force. No one was entirely sure what either Gorbachev or the junta leaders would do.

To keep to my planned schedule I kept my morning visit to the White House brief and hurried across town to the Library of Foreign Literature to give a lecture at 10:00 A.M. on the relationship of libraries to democracy. I was amazed and delighted to see Ivanov there waiting to introduce me, having come directly once again from an all-night vigil at the White House with his son. Drawing on the second wind that the best Russian intellectuals always seem to find in times of crisis, Ivanov turned the discussion period into a virtuoso evocation of the Russia that might have been had not the rich promise of the early-twentieth-century been wiped out by Communism.

Ivanov began with the story of perhaps the greatest of all scholar-librarians, the ascetic Nicholas Fedorov, who had directed the Rumiantsev Museum (later Lenin Library), had brought scientists and humanists together, and had given the enterprise of learning a literally cosmic dimension. Ivanov told how the selfless Fedorov had decisively influenced the great pioneer of space rocketry, Konstanin Tsiolkovsky. Because he was hard of hearing, Tsiolkovsky had fallen behind in his studies. Fedorov patiently tutored him in reading and imparted to him the idea of probing and colonizing outer space in order to accommodate the overcrowding of the earth, which Fedorov believed would result from the imminent large-scale resurrection of the dead. The visionary Fedorov passionately believed that modern science would soon make this ancient Christian idea possible, if humanity would replace its fratricidal warfare with this "common task."

Ivanov used the Fedorov–Tsiolkovsky connection to illustrate the practical benefits that came from visionary ideas in pre-Soviet Russia. He then used the example of the great mathematician Andrei Kolmogorov to show how the Soviet system had failed to derive practical benefit even from those scientists it did not persecute. Kolmogorov's statistical work demonstrated already by the late 1930s that the daily computation of possible production mistakes at the smallest units of production would enable any manufacturing process to make instant corrections that would increase both the quality and the economy of output. But it was only in Japan many years later that his idea was applied.

Ivanov then went on to discuss the neglected implications of the ideas of the chemist Vladimir Vernadsky and the economist Nikolai Kondratieff. Vernadsky, like Kolmogorov and Sakharov, illustrated for Ivanov the Russian belief in a unified and infinitely expanding, but always humane, scientific culture. Ivanov seemed to suggest that the events in Moscow were a kind of vindication of Vernadsky's idea that humanity was on the verge of moving from the domain of biological processes to one controlled by human consciousness.

The example of Kondratieff inspired the implicit challenge that Ivanov made at the end to his fascinated audience. Ivanov pointed out that periods of war and economic crisis were—in Kondratieff's famous theory of cycles—precisely the periods in which new ideas and fresh creativity came into flower. Ivanov's understated improvisation seemed to suggest that Russia would have to compensate for the inevitable material hardships that now lay ahead with new efforts in the life of the mind.

Listening to Ivanov speak without notes and without sleep, I felt I was witnessing a living illustration of man's higher faculties triumphing over his lower ones. My thoughts went back to the first time I met Ivanov almost exactly twenty-five years earlier in the kitchen of Nadezhda Mandelshtam. The roundtable discussions that were going on almost continuously in Ivanov's library reminded me of the intense meetings that used to take place over a cup of tea with Mandelshtam. She had told me the last time I ever saw her that "Koma," as his friends called him, was quite simply "the shining hope" (*blesk i nadezhda*) of the Russian future. What we heard that morning from Ivanov was the digested version of a spectacular series of lectures he had given the previous year at Moscow University to an audience of more than a thousand. Earlier in his career he had been thrown out of Moscow University for defending Pasternak, and he was hounded for years by the Communist Party establishment for befriending and standing by other victims of persecution. He had used his ostracism to travel to remote places and study the languages of small minority groups. When he became head of the Library of Foreign Literature, once run by former Prime Minister Aleksei Kosygin's untalented daughter, it was said that someone who knew no languages had been succeeded by someone who knew them all.

Ivanov had added the language of politics to his repertoire as a recently elected People's Deputy of the USSR. The Yeltsin forces had picked him to help conduct their difficult negotiations with Lukianov in the Kremlin on August 20. In the evening, Ivanov used his linguistic ability to answer questions about what was going on via international telephone with media from many countries in a variety of languages. I was later told that his conversations with the Portuguese-speaking world were particularly important. Portuguese television recorded the fullest and most graphic shots of the killing of the three young men, and much of the best coverage of the period was from smaller, non-English-speaking countries that were in direct touch by phone with people like Ivanov.

As the seminar drew to a close, I remembered having suggested in my lecture at this same library just before the coup that Russia's future would be determined by which of two types of catharsis the Russian people would experience in reconstructing their society. Would it be a traditional, imperial catharsis based on purges, scapegoats, and negative

63

nationalism or a deeper, moral catharsis that involved the rebirth of conscience and the transcending of violence? Returning now for a second roundtable less than a week later, it seemed hard to believe that Russia had moved from a crude attempt at the former to a seeming victory of the latter.

Most remarkable of all in the decisive forty-eight hours had been the absence of violence on the part of the Yeltsin forces, who were constantly lecturing their followers on and beyond the barricades to avoid provocations. They seem to have fired no shots and to have thrown Molotov cocktails only at the tank that killed two of the young men. The young people on the barricades were, as one young woman put it, "not cattle to be coerced." They saw the troops facing them as converts to be convinced and the putsch leaders as criminals to be confined. Spontaneous and disorganized as the crowds had been, there was very little random violence or demand for revenge.

By the early afternoon of August 21, the rumors in Moscow began to focus on the escape plans, rather than the assault plans, of the junta. The library conference was getting ready to go to a formal reception in a place that no one would have believed even a few hours ago would be open to the public: the Kremlin itself. Not only was this former headquarters of many of the key conspirators thrown open, it was transformed by normally reserved librarians into a place of festivity. The usual kitsch background band of balalaika-strumming folksingers in pseudo-peasant costumes suddenly came alive, and our largely middle-aged and overweight international company formed a giant chorus line that went snaking out through the solemn and impersonal Palace of Congresses.

I felt almost sorry for sympathizers with the coup like Shuvalov, who appeared nervous at the reception and anxious to have himself photographed with Western librarians.

Others, like Zakharov, seemed to be suggesting that they could survive a tactical retreat. *"Ya voenny"* ("I am a military man"), he explained with a semi-shrug and a resigned but not defeated look.

The high point of the reception came after about an hour of festivities when the group I had left the night before suddenly showed up from the barricades. None of them had slept, but they were happy people, and it was a joy and a privilege to share in the bear hugs. I was happiest of all to see our man in Moscow, Mikhail Levner, still wearing the bright red Library of Congress T-shirt and jogging pants that he had worn all night on the barricades. He had been my efficient and cheerful companion ever since my arrival, but he had a devastated look on his face when he left my hotel room late on the first night of the coup with the simple words *tiazhely den* ("a heavy day").

After an exhausting schedule of calls with me and chores for other Library of Congress colleagues the following day, Levner had quietly headed off—as I should have known he would—to make his own stand on the barricades at the time the attack was expected in the evening of of August 20. He was collecting leaflets and broadsides for our collections even as he formed part of the human wall. "I did it," he later quietly explained to me, "for our motherland," using the intimate word *rodina*. It was a moving affirmation of patriotism by one who has never been able to get even a minimally decent apartment for his family and whose people have not been all that well treated by many who called themselves Russian patriots. But the patriotism of the barricades, like the Yeltsin entourage inside the White House, was more ethnically diverse than is generally realized, and the comradeship there seemed to offer some hope that new democratic ideals might transcend old animosities.

There was a final scare—never, as far as I am aware, reported in the press. At 6:30 A.M. on Thursday, August 22, about sixty people in civilian clothes and carrying firearms suddenly gathered in front of the largely undefended White House. A number of other armed personnel also appeared on the roofs of nearby houses. An alert was sounded inside the White House, and a miniversion of the human wall was formed outside. The armed group then vanished as rapidly and mysteriously as it had appeared.[29]

One reason that there may have been a tentative last effort to penetrate the White House at that hour was that the armored units protecting Yeltsin had just left. I saw them filing out of Moscow along Lenin Prospect as I was being interviewed by Ted Koppel for *Nightline* on the tiny balcony of the ABC television office. I had had very little sleep for three straight nights and was immediately told by the cameraman to lean far out over the rickety railing in order to make a better picture. But I was grateful for the chance to describe something of what was happening, and I felt better as soon as I looked down, despite my congenital fear of heights. New tricolor Russian flags were fluttering from the turrets of the departing tanks directly beneath us, and one young soldier waved a flower at an old woman who was sweeping the street.

A festive spirit developed once again in Moscow during the daytime of August 22. After participating in yet another set of discussions at the Library of Foreign Literature, I blended with Misha Levner into a swelling crowd that converged on the headquarters of the Central Committee of the Communist Party just beyond Red Square. All of Moscow, it seemed, now wanted to participate in the transformation that only a few had helped start at the White House. But, once again, the crowd was keeping both internal discipline and a clear political objective. Everyone knew by then that Pugo had committed suicide, that the rest of the junta was being arrested, and that the entire Leninist machine had been deeply involved—the Communist Party apparatus as well as the KGB. Both the Moscow city government and Yeltsin's Russian Republic had decreed the confiscation of Communist Party property. Once official signs saying "sealed and untouchable" (*opechatanno*) were placed on all the buildings of the Central Committee, the crowd moved on with almost no vandalism to the large open square in front of the three massive buildings that made up the central headquarters of the KGB.

One or two windows were smashed on the ground floor of the main building, the infamous Lubyanka prison, but such actions were immediately curtailed by the crowd, which soon turned its attention to the giant 14-ton statue of Feliks Dzerzhinsky, the founder of the Soviet secret police, in the middle of the square. After decorating it with slogans and tricolor banners, the crowd made some amateur and unsuccessful efforts to topple it. A loudspeaker truck soon arrived bearing the youthful voice of the deputy mayor of Moscow, Sergei Stankevich, who assured the crowd that the monument "will be leveled" (*budet sniat, budet sniat* had both a decisive and a derisive ring), but that massive technical expertise was needed and that the crowd should stand back and not interfere: "We lost only three people in defending democracy; we must not lose anyone while dismantling the dictatorship."

After a while, four giant cranes arrived bearing prominent Krupp labels. Clearly highlighted by the setting sun, they began a long series of swinging movements over the statue like a family of thin-necked brontosauruses slowly closing in on their evening meal. Cables were eventually secured under the head and arms of "Iron Feliks" and the statue was neatly lifted off its pedestal. During the long wait for that moment, a festive but remarkably orderly atmosphere prevailed among the crowd of some 50,000.

As I listened to the familiar democratic leaders recycle the speeches they had previously given at the White House,

I realized how profoundly the rhetoric of Russia had been transformed in these few days. Gone was not just the hackneyed language of Communist propaganda but also the self-indulgent pomposities of the Moscow intelligentsia and of the new democratic politicans themselves. In campaign speeches and particularly in the parliaments of the USSR, there had developed during the preceding two years a tendency to wallow at great length in denouncing past errors with a mixture of self-pity and self-righteousness, omitting any realistic discussion of remedies. Speeches at the White House and now in Dzerzhinsky Square tended to be short, self-effacing, and focused on specifics.

These were the expectations that the crowd had unconsciously developed for speakers by the time the loudspeaker announced that it was about to transmit the live broadcast of Gorbachev's press conference, his first direct interaction with the Russian people since returning just before dawn from his Crimean captivity.

This was a major moment. The rank-and-file friends of reform had found their dislike and distrust of Gorbachev deepening during the past year. They were not reassured when, upon his arrival at Vnukovo Airport early that morning, he had recycled his own favorite slogan to describe the defeat of the coup as "a victory of perestroika." But pictures spoke more powerfully than words at such an emotional time, and most Russians were moved by the obvious suffering on Gorbachev's face in the televised images of his descent from the plane. The reformers had made his return to office a key point in their demands and were anxious to hear if there was a new Gorbachev to speak to their new condition.

Unfortunately, it was still the old Gorbachev. His lengthy introductory account of his own ordeal held their interest for a while, but he soon lost them with his lawyerly manner, his self-justifying tone, and his assumption that the

Communist Party as such would not be implicated. The silence of the crowd around me was finally broken when he used one of his characteristically solemn and vague formulations to say that there were undoubtedly important lessons to be learned in this experience "for everyone." "Except him," said one Russian who had been on the barricades. Mutterings of annoyance began to spread.

When the first questioner asked him in a genuinely perplexed and nonconfrontational way why in the world Gorbachev had ever hired all the people who had made the putsch, he simply evaded the question rather than expose all the inner questioning that he himself must have been experiencing. Instead, he gave a long, self-serving account of his own reform program, filled with formulaic language about "stages in the development of perestroika."[30] People began whistling in derision. After his discourse was completed without ever answering the question, the crowd called out "turn it off." The loudspeaker cut off its transmission of the rest of Gorbachev's press conference to what must have been its largest single live audience.

Gorbachev did not realize that the fever had broken. The patient was beginning to get well on his own. He no longer wanted a witch doctor muttering formulas or needed to be told not to start a witch hunt. That was precisely the gratuitous advice which Gorbachev proceeded to offer the Russian people in the subsequent part of his press conference, which fortunately for him had been cut off from transmission in Dzerzhinsky Square. The Russian people wanted renewal, not revenge. But it was still All-Hallows Eve for Gorbachev, who seemed to be haunted by the ghosts of witches past and not yet in tune with those who had exorcised them.

The tension was to get still worse between Gorbachev and the reformers before he was able to share with them in a kind of All-Saints Day: the funeral on Saturday of the three young men who had died on the barricades. But those three intervening days put him through a different kind of purgatory from the one he had experienced in his Crimean captivity. For those were the days in which he (and much of the West, which still looked at Russia through his eyes) slowly came to realize that something truly unique was happening in this country. It was a case not just of power transferred, but of people transformed.

There was remarkably little melodrama about the toppling of Dzerzhinsky's monument. Contrary to many people's expectations, it did not lead to an epidemic of desecrations in Moscow. Only a very small flag was placed on the empty pedestal, a rather modest reminder of the fact that the tricolor had been named the official flag by the Russian parliament earlier in the day. This was not the stuff of a Delacroix painting, but it was part of the continuing originality and improvisation that was transforming a country.

As I left Dzerzhinsky square with Misha and wandered through the dark streets of the relatively unchanged old city, more lines came back to me from Pasternak: "Moscow met me in the darkness / which somehow turned to silver"

Skvoz proshlogo peripetii	Through the troubles of the past
I gody voin i nishchety	And years of war and poverty
Ya molcha uznaval rossii	I silently began to understand
Nepoftorimye cherty.[31]	The unrepeatable traits of Russia.

We were on our way to my next scheduled event, a reception at the State Historical Library. Reputed to be a center of reform and innovation, this was the one great Moscow library I had never visited. As we wended our way there through deserted back streets of the old city, we passed a synagogue. I asked if we could go in. After Misha spoke with the curator and I placed a Kleenex on my head in lieu of a yarmulke, we entered the worn but majestic building. It was awe-inspiring to see in the near darkness a series of old world balconies jutting out into the worship space beneath the high ceiling. The curator explained that it used to be a yeshiva and library as well as a temple and that they were beginning to restore it to that former state. "Perhaps things will move faster now," he said quietly as we were leaving.

An unusually large number of librarians from the national republics were at the Historical Library, and it was reassuring to see them sharing in the joy of their Russian colleagues at the outcome of the crisis. The youthful staff served us all sweet, Soviet champagne and engaged us in the same kind of earnest talk about computers and information systems that I had heard among so many of the young professionals on the barricades. One sensed in the director, Mikhail Afanasev, the information professional of the future, even as one recognized in him the historian's genuine commitment to preserving the past.

As I was preparing to leave the Historical Library, the sky suddenly lit up with fireworks. They had been set off all over Moscow to celebrate the end of the crisis. Through the large windows of the reading room used for the reception I could see the nearby silhouette of a beautiful onion-domed church of the late Muscovite period. I was delighted to discover amidst these young people a church that I had never seen before from my favorite period of historical study. It seemed a perfect final vignette for a historian to take away from a day of celebration. I carried this picture home in my mind and happily to bed. Not until the morning after did I learn that this picturesque church was a confiscated building, still being used as a storehouse for confiscated books housed under derelict conditions and not accessible to the public.

A sense of the immensity of what was still needed to make real changes in the system pressed in on me on Friday, August 23, the last day of the library conference. The little world of libraries mirrored the larger political world of the USSR, where the central jurisdiction of all-union authorities was being questioned in the Russian parliament, and where the national republics were beginning to feel some apprehension about the Russian resurgence under Yeltsin. At breakfast, the head of the second largest library in the USSR, the Saltykov-Shchedrin in Leningrad, argued that his institution should formally become the national library of the Russian Republic and thus, presumably, recapture the role it had enjoyed as the imperial library before 1917. Several Russian parliamentarians spoke about the need of their overheated legislature for a library; reformers in the all-union parliament and in the nearly independent Baltic republics were asking for the same thing; and the reformist mayor of Moscow seemed to be picking up the imprisoned Boldin's idea of a Book Academy. But there was no money for any of this, and existing libraries were continuing to disintegrate.

The final meeting of the library conference on Friday, August 24, had a celebratory but somewhat surreal quality. Foreigners who had previously been afraid to speak up now lavishly praised the victory of Russian democracy, while Russian officials who appeared to have favored the other side took the bows. I felt a certain sympathy for the head of the Lenin Library, Anatoly Volik, when I went to see him the day before I left to discuss the conference that the Library of Congress was organizing with him in Moscow for late October. He and his senior staff had already done exhaustive work to host the August conference. Now many people were talking as if his great national library should be either bypassed or broken up like other all-union enterprises.

To be sure, Volik's name had not been on the list of five candidates that a special scholarly committee had recommended for the Lenin Library job, and the absence of unclassified writing from his credits suggested that he—like many in the information business of the USSR—had a background in security rather than in bibliographical services. But I believed that he was genuinely trying to save a great institution and that his background in automation could be useful in that cause. He noted wearily to me on Friday afternoon that it was difficult to work in a society where "people think one thing, say another, and do a third." I was sitting in his office in the giant main building of the Lenin Library, which was said to be slowly sinking into the newly constructed Borovitskaia metro station. We were making plans for its weeklong joint conference with the Library of Congress in October. That gathering subsequently proved to be the most candid and inclusive discussion of the importance of libraries for democratic development that I have ever experienced in the USSR. Volik deserved much of the credit; and it saddened me to learn later that the world's second largest library had to be shut down altogether in November and was reopened early in 1992 by borrowing from a commercial bank and bringing in a new director.

One of the most interesting people to appear at the Library of Congress–Lenin Library conference in October 1991 was the former head of the political section of the state censorship office, Vladimir Solodin. This meek-looking, round-faced figure argued that the attempt to restore order by the Extraordinary Situation Committee was not a putsch at all: "The real putsch was Yeltsin's drive for power that followed." The "so-called coup d'état" was, in fact, a provocation designed to justify the premeditated dismantling of Communist rule. The real villain was Gorbachev, who simply sat there "bare-assed on a snowdrift" (*golym zadom na sugrob*) as the USSR spiraled downward into anarchy. The inevitable, eventual outcome, he felt, would be a new dictatorship, probably led by Yeltsin himself.

There was, already in those heady late days of August 1991, some reason for concern about Yeltsin's ultimate aspirations after his stunning victory. He made some unfortunate remarks about the possibility of adjusting borders with other republics to incorporate ethnic Russians into his domain. At times he seemed impatient with Gorbachev during his marathon session before the Russian parliament on Thursday morning, August 22.

But Yeltsin's government seemed to most Russians I talked with at the time more measured and moderate than it looked to most foreign diplomats and journalists. Once the threat of a coup had passed, the West seemed to shift its attention back to the familiar figure of Gorbachev and on to the new drama of national republics straining toward independence. Having generally treated Yeltsin patronizingly in the past, the West now found it easy to assume that he would ride roughshod over both the resurrection of Gorbachev and the birth of new nations. Thus, an academic on the MacNeil/Lehrer show spoke of Yeltsin's "fascist side" and was not seriously challenged,[32] while print journalism followed the lead of the *New York Times* front page, which depicted Yeltsin pointing menacingly at Gorbachev and described how an "abusive audience" "scorned" and "heckled" him in the Russian Parliament.[33]

In point of fact, Yeltsin's Russian government had been dealing with the other republics on a basis of parity for some time. Almost all the representatives of other republics I met at the time through the library conference praised Yeltsin for saving them from the imperial reconsolidation that the junta planned and were more worried about Gorbachev's desire to reconsolidate the union than about imperial tendencies in Yeltsin.

Moreover, the Russians with whom I watched the Gorbachev visit to the Russian parliament on television thought it mainly illustrated Gorbachev's continued insensitivity to the changes that had taken place in his absence. In the famous picture, Yeltsin was pointing not at Gorbachev personally but at the bundle of laws he had just given Gorbachev that had been passed by the Russian parliament during the coup attempt. It was an important constitutional gesture on the part of a lower authority toward a superior one who had not acknowledged it. Although there were indeed some tense and even rude moments, Yeltsin ended the visit with warm words for Gorbachev and a gracious invitation to return in the future when all were more rested, which was never reported in the West.

Far more important than the interplay between Yeltsin and Gorbachev was the struggle going on within the emerging new generation of Russian leaders to fill the void left by the collapse of Communism and to define a new identity for the Russian people. I had indicated in my lecture on this subject just a week before the coup that the contest was between an autocratic nationalism imposed from the top down, seeing the state and army as the heart of the Russian experience, and a new kind of democratic identity developed from the bottom up, based on a market economy and a nongovernmental civil society.

Yeltsin's defeat of the junta represented a clear victory of the latter over the former concept, but there was at least a trace of each idea within each camp. The junta's stated desire was to restore order so that democratic reforms could continue; their model appears to have been a South Korea or Chile, where strong rule was combined with an open market economy rather than a totally closed society. The Yeltsin camp aimed to transfer most central power from the union to the Russian republic rather than to dissolve it altogether, and Yeltsin's leadership often seemed authoritarian in style even though democratic in content.

I went to the dedication of a new French Cultural Center within Ivanov's Library of Foreign Literature late on Friday afternoon. In a long conversation with me and the French Ambassador, Ivanov expressed both political and personal concern about Gorbachev's psychological condition. I resolved that he should talk with our new Ambassador, Bob Strauss, whom I had agreed to see the next morning before he was to present his credentials to Gorbachev. When I introduced him to Strauss early the next morning, Ivanov gave a brilliant exposition of the depth of change that had occurred in Russia. He stressed, on the one hand, the human need to reassure Gorbachev that he was not alone and had a secure place in history and, on the other, the political need to persuade Gorbachev to break completely with Communism if he intends to continue playing a constructive role in the national leadership. Bob Strauss listened closely, taking notes on an envelope. I had the feeling that his considerable political energies were focusing with renewed intensity on his forthcoming meeting. The Ambassador invited me to accompany him to Manezh Square, where he visited briefly with Gorbachev before delivering a well-received short message from President Bush at the memorial service for the three young men killed on the barricades.

I stood close to Gorbachev for much of that ceremony and talked briefly with him once. He still had something of the hunted and haunted look that he had shown upon his arrival back from the Crimea. But he also seemed less pompous and more human than on previous occasions. He was not the featured speaker and did not get the most applause, but he used the word transformation (*preobrazovanie*) to describe what had happened in Russia in a context where he would previously have used perestroika; and he choked up briefly when he first mentioned the fallen young men.

He was beginning to extract his humanity from the wreckage of the Leninist machine, and he was soon to free it further from the chauvinist temptation. Later that day in the Kremlin, Gorbachev was visited by his old military adviser and the senior surviving military leader in the USSR, Marshal Akhromeev. Stripped of his pistol on the way in because of suspected complicity in the plot, this aging hero from World War II apparently received no satisfaction from Gorbachev that the disintegration of Communist central rule would be arrested. He left and hanged himself immediately. He left behind a note declaring that everything he had lived for was being destroyed.

With ordinary Russians discovering the power that hope can bring, this extraordinary Russian had lost the hope that power had provided. When I heard on Sunday about Akhromeev's fate, my thoughts went back to my last conversation with him at a buffet given by Ben Bradlee of the *Washington Post* a year before. The conversation, which included a sizable segment of the American foreign policy establishment, had rambled amiably back and forth between broad platitudes about peace and narrow questions about arms control. I inadvertently spoiled the party by asking the Marshal about his role as a deputy of the Supreme Soviet representing the restless Moldavian republic. "They are all nationalists, extremists," he sputtered. When I mentioned the name of another of the deputies from Moldavia, the liberal writer Ion Drutse, he got even angrier, denouncing subversive elements seeking to break up the USSR. He clearly liked his colleague even less than his constituents—in fact he had little use for democratic legislatures in general, where "little people make much noise."

But between August 19 and 24, 1991, the little people had begun to make themselves heard in Moscow even more clearly than in Moldavia. Russia had not yet found itself, but its consciousness had been transformed. A new generation was taking over, and both Yeltsin and Gorbachev were being swept into its quest for a new beginning.

77

PART THREE

Transformation

◈ 6 ◈

The Voice from Within

After the funeral on Saturday, August 24, for the three young men killed at the underpass, Gorbachev resigned as General Secretary of the Communist Party of the Soviet Union. In his governmental capacity as President, he then ordered the confiscation of all Communist Party property. Those possessions, in fact, had already been largely taken over by the Russian and other republic and local governments, but the decision by the head of the once all-controlling Leninist Party to "surrender those powers" and to dissolve the Party's controlling structures marked the formal end of Communist rule in the Soviet version of the Russian empire.

In *What Is to be Done?*, the founding document of the Communist Party written in 1903, Lenin had insisted that the "consciousness" of an elite organization was necessary to give discipline and focus to the confused "spontaneity" of working people struggling for revolutionary change in Russia. Eighty-eight years later, spontaneity struck back to destroy this self-perpetuating elite and to create a new consciousness of its own. In his brief televised address to the nation, Gorbachev confirmed that this was, indeed, a "transformation" and not just another "stage of perestroika." Having let go of the last Leninist slogan, he was urging his fellow Communists to discard the illusion of a superior consciousness and to blend back into the spontaneous "renewal of society" by "joining actively in the continuation of radical democratic transformations in the interests of working people."[34]

A resurgence of spontaneity from the bottom up had undermined Communist rule from the top down in Eastern Europe. Solidarity in Poland was the pathbreaking movement.[35] Although its nonviolent, mass-based struggle against Leninist machine rule had been brutally suppressed by the imposition of martial law in December 1981, Solidarity quietly gained new authority in the course of the 1980s. It began reconstructing from below a democratic consciousness that gained control of the government once the Communist Party itself opened the floodgates of reform. Uncontainable spontaneity destroyed the Leninist political machines of Eastern Europe in 1989, and the contagion spread to Russia as workers and intellectuals began to work together there as well when a measure of genuine choice was permitted in the elections of 1990.

Yeltsin's spontaneity, as much as his courage, enabled him to become the magnetic pole that pulled isolated scraps of metalic resistance from all over Moscow toward his iron bar of new authority. Yevtushenko was drawn into the resistance by Yeltsin's simple, almost joyful manner "in the frighteningly empty corridors of power" on August 19. "Like in fairy tale . . . he absolutely bought my heart."[36] Among all the celebrities that joined the resistance, Mstislav Rostropovich made by far the greatest impression, largely because of the spontaneity of his gesture: simply getting on a plane in Paris, barging through customs without a visa, and remaining by Yeltsin's side.[37] In the instant television epics that mythologized the events, there were almost always freeze frames of Rostropovich broadly smiling from the White House balcony with his hands joined over his head. In a society where all social movement had been to some extent coercive and planned, the defense of the White House was a spontaneous and voluntary undertaking.

Gorbachev himself seemed to catch the spirit of spontaneity when he opened the all-union Supreme Soviet on Monday, August 26, by freely acknowledging something he had been avoiding in the aftermath of his return:

> They say that I have come back to a different country. I agree with this. A man came back to a different country—and now looks upon everything—the past, the present, and the future—with different eyes.[38]

Gorbachev's resistance to the putsch and his new decision to press on with radical democratic reform free of Communism represented important contributions to the transformation of Russia. Yet the new Gorbachev was not applauded any more in his own all-union parliament than the old Gorbachev had been the previous week in Yeltsin's Russian parliament. And the reason was not simply past resentment or rivalry with Yeltsin. It was just that no political functionary from the old order could quite be trusted without the new credentials of having put one's life on the line in the Moscow events of August.

I asked one of the Yeltsin aides who was relatively sympathetic to Gorbachev if he did not think Gorbachev's conversion was important for Russia. "It is important for *him*," my friend replied. And this was exactly the same answer to the question I asked another veteran of the White House resistance about what seemed to me the considerable significance of the Orthodox Patriarch's endorsement of the Yeltsin cause when the outcome hung in the balance. Yes, my friend said calmly, it was important "for *him.*"

My friends seemed to be suggesting that the heads of both state and church were to be judged by something higher than either of their domains: by the voice of conscience. Only by responding affirmatively to that inner voice could those necessarily implicated in the repression and deception of the past re-equip themselves to speak for and to the new Russia.

In my talk on "Russia in Search of Itself," I had put heavy emphasis on the point President Václav Havel of Czechoslovakia had made in his address to a joint session of Congress in February 1991: that everyone who lives in a totalitarian system—even those like him who were jailed for their resistance—shares some complicity in its web of repression. The rebirth of individual conscience was the key to breaking free of that web, and one of the better journalistic reprises on the week of the coup aptly described it as creating "a crucible of conscience."[39]

If the physical resistance had necessarily been the work of only a few in Moscow, the crisis of conscience was something that almost everyone in Russia had to confront directly. In a society where one had survived by avoiding responsibility, everyone was forced to make public moral choices. They faced small decisions of what to say over dinner or at work about the two rival governments claiming their allegiance: the all-union junta and the Russian resistance. They faced bigger decisions about whether to speak out, do anything about it, or join in active resistance. Legal proceedings and judgments would come later, but a higher standard of moral accountability was already lifting people's sights beyond a thirst for revenge to the possibility of renewal. People continued to examine the signs of weakness they had noted in themselves during the time of trial and continued to blame others not so much for what they had done as for the absence of conscience exemplified in their subsequent behavior. Yeltsin likened the conspirators' tendency to turn on each other rather than accept blame themselves to cockroaches eating each other up in a bottle.

The surgeon Yury Sidorenko, an articulate Yeltsinite in the Russian parliament, has described in detail the special kind of anger he and his fellow defenders of the White House felt at the argumentation offered just after the events by those who did not support the resistance. In both the Russian Supreme Soviet and the Congress of People's Deputies, delegates used legal technicalities, academic arguments, and bureaucratic rationalizations to avoid any acceptance of personal accountability. Sidorenko was outraged not because he wanted those figures punished but because he wanted them to acknowledge the moral dimension involved in political choices. He found only a type of personality "absolutely devoid of conscience," using arguments that were "forged from start to finish," and falling back as a last resort on "a voice of contrition with a skimpy and discordant pronunciation."[40]

Yet conscience had been at work in many ways short of full contrition. For many there was moral emancipation in merely speaking out or standing up at a meeting; for others in signing a petition, sewing together a tricolor, or cooking the *pirozhki* that were taken to the barricades. And in the confused camp of the putschists themselves, there was moral growth in the refusal of some to obey orders—and of others to give them. Was it Pavlov's wife or Pavlov himself—or a little bit of both—that heard the inner voice and refrained from ever issuing the order to open fire?

Russians had discovered that decent human relations required the recovery of a moral vocabulary. The power of conscience had broken out of its confinement within a great literature and the private deliberations of an intelligentsia.

Conscience had been activated on the barricades, and it was being stimulated by a newly liberated television and radio. Russia was finding its inner voice. In my final talk at the Library of Foreign Literature on Monday, August 26, I told the gathering what a great privilege it had been to be in their midst during a period of moral rebirth.[41] It was inspiring to think that "the all-human values" Russians had articulated in their nineteenth-century literature might yet be brought to bear on their twentieth-century politics.

After nearly a millennium of relative silence, Russia found its literary voice in the nineteenth century, bringing to European literary forms the moral passion and religious intensity of a semimedieval society just entering its age of humanism. Russian literature was penetrated by a sense of moral responsibility: to one's better self, to one's family, and to the *narod* (in both its meanings—the people and the nation). Tolstoy sought to root man's moral responsibility in the rediscovery of the pantheistic natural world; Dostoevsky, in a rediscovered Christianity. But almost all Russian literary figures believed that morality was universal and not merely tribal, based on something transcendent and not merely utilitarian.

The deep humanism of Russian literature was bitterly attacked by the debunking materialism of Russian radical criticism as depicted in Turgenev's *Fathers and Sons*. But the "all-human values" of the great Russian novels were reaffirmed and enriched by a new explosion of idealistic philosophical, theological, and poetic literature in the last years of Tsarist rule before the victory of the deterministic Marxist materialism, which provided the foundation for Soviet totalitarianism. By rediscovering the rich, long-supressed legacy of this "Silver Age," young Russians were finding philosophical roots for their reformist impulses.

I left Russia before dawn on Tuesday, August 27. The logistical crew of the Congress of Compatriots sent a huge bus to take me to the airport. I felt awkward in using it for one person, and the driver was furious at having been awakened so early. But he was also well into the new market economics and was willing to make the trip in exchange for a substantial bribe. The tireless Misha accompanied me to Sheremetevo airport, where I piled through the lines into the antiseptic world of duty-free shops and a faded Pan Am flight back to America.

Decompressing from the most exhilarating experience of my life, I remembered a great lecture from my student days by Walter Phelps (Buzzer) Hall, who described Giuseppe Garibaldi during the Revolution of 1848, standing alone for the freedom of his people on the Janiculan Hill in Rome against all the armed forces of Europe closing in on him. In the short run, Garibaldi was defeated; but his cause eventually prevailed, and Hall concluded the lecture with a line that came back to me as I thought about how the Yeltsin White House had activated the hitherto purely cerebral conscience of Russia: "Not in flight of thought, but in action lies freedom."

And yet the Russians' action, rooted as it was in conscience, was giving rise to new thoughts—thoughts unclouded by the rationalizations and dogmatic formulae of the past. Russians were thinking seriously about problems that had not been on their agenda before: how to organize a democracy, how to decentralize power, how to recognize diversity, and how to privatize an economy. All these issues would take many painful years to resolve, and there could be drastic setbacks as well as surprising progress along the way. But it seemed clear to me that there was a new basic mentality, which had been growing for a long time and was now crystallized into solid form by these events.

Wilhelm Dilthey contended that humanity had produced only three basic types of world view: the objective idealists, the naturalists, and the idealists of freedom. Each view had its own philosophical assumptions, historical adherents, and psychological satisfactions. Russia, I thought in the darkness of that bus rattling toward the airport, long believed in the idealism of divinely sanctioned monarchy, which had been replaced by the materialism of an atheistic absolutism. Now at last they had produced idealists of freedom to whom the hope of the future belonged.

No one could say how, when—or perhaps even whether—Russia would be transformed into some kind of democratic state. But it was clear that they now had the agent for transformation: a strong cadre of battle-tested individuals who believed that the worth and grandeur of man depended on his free, individual response to the voice of conscience within, rather than on collective obedience to the megaphones of authority from without.

7

Meditations on the Matroshka

The long flight back enabled me to reflect as a historian on events I had seen as a witness. I felt I could discern a certain similarity between the unexpected transformation of Eastern Europe in 1989–91 and the equally unanticipated revolutions of 1848–50 in Europe.

In the conservative, seemingly stable Europe of the 1840s, unrest that previously might have been localized suddenly spread like a contagious disease through the revolutionary new means of communication: telegraphic wires and high-speed printing presses. Karl Marx, the greatest revolutionary of that era, had moved to Brussels, the city in which the wires of the three great services, Reuters, Havas, and Wolff, were about to converge and be connected. Marx organized his first "Communist Correspondence Committee" essentially within the communications industry there. So central were his journalistic activity and connections to his early revolutionary organizations that a recent student of the period has suggested that his League of Communists should more properly be called "the party of the *Neue Rheinische Zeitung*."[42]

In his Communist Manifesto, published just two weeks before the revolutions of 1848 broke out, Marx wrongly predicted that national sentiment would die out in the revolutionary struggle. But he rightly saw that a rising tide of reformism brought about by economic change would lead to a genuinely revolutionary uprising.

In the equally conservative Europe of the 1960s, another communication revolution was preparing the way for a fresh contagion of unrest, borne this time by television, tape recorders, and samizdat. Official Russia in the 1960s no less than in the 1840s was the backbone of conservative resistance to change in Europe, and it intervened militarily to repress democratization in Czechoslovakia in 1968 as it had in Hungary in 1849 (and again in 1956).

In the 1960s as in the 1840s, Russia was too far away and too strictly controlled for its young people to share in the revolutionary activity and enthusiasm of their European contemporaries. But in both cases, thinking Russians were deeply interested in such movements of change. Once their own repressive government suffered defeat in a war (Crimea in 1855, Afghanistan in 1989) and embarked on a program of Westernizing reform, a truly radical youth movement arose that was totally determined to transform the system.

Then as now, the ruling Russian authorities no less than the watching Western world seriously underestimated the pent-up intensity of a rising new generation. Alexander II, the most liberal of all Russian rulers, came to be resented and rejected by young people, whose expectations he had aroused but could not satisfy. Gorbachev told me in a conversation during the Moscow summit meetings in June 1988 that Alexander II was one of his two models from prerevolutionary Russia (Peter the Great was the other). The impatience with a reformist Gorbachev among precisely those young people who were benefiting most from his changes often seemed reminiscent of that earlier revolution of rising expectations under a reforming Alexander II.

Alexander II in his early years liberalized press censorship, Westernized the legal order, and introduced local self-government. But the liberal reforms championed by his generation only intensified the desire for total change by the next.

Gorbachev likewise Westernized the political order by introducing real elections for real legislatures and by radically liberalizing the media under glasnost. But, by early 1991, Gorbachev had—like Alexander II late in his reign—lost almost all of his initial domestic support and was admired mainly abroad.

I wondered on the long return flight from Moscow about how similar or different their fates might prove to be. Alexander II was finally assassinated and succeeded by a reactionary rule that both delayed and deepened the final revolutionary crisis. Would Gorbachev, whose domestic popularity was in free fall even below his pitiful pre-coup 14 percent acceptance rating, suffer political if not physical extinction—and perhaps ultimately also be succeeded by some form of even more authoritarian rule?

This was the secret hope of many in the Russian military–industrial complex and in the Leninist political machine, and it was the fearful expectation of many in the West who identified the prospects for reform in Russia with the political fate of Gorbachev.

But more is involved in great processes of change than mere personalities. In some respects, Alexander II was a more remarkable reformer than Gorbachev, because he initiated a real transformation of the society by liberating the serfs. Gorbachev, for all his talk of restructuring, never gave his "serfs" on the collective farms even the limited freedom that the Chinese Communists had granted. History, however did not depend on Gorbachev to initiate a social revolution. One had already taken place.

The rise to maturity of an educated postwar, post-Stalinist generation is the fundamental sociopolitical change that Gorbachev, Yeltsin, and all other political figures of the older, sixty-plus generation have had to deal with. The most important government-initiated social change in the USSR during the postwar era was the ending of the large-scale gulag system by an otherwise repressive and neo-Leninist Nikita Khrushchev. Gorbachev, whose political apprenticeship occurred in the Khrushchev era, was in some respects shaped by the brief but hopeful post-Stalinist "thaw," during which he studied law at Moscow University. He became the first university-educated person ever to rule Russia (with the first university-educated wife of a leader to assume a public role on her own). He brought the new educated, professional class into the political arena by creating an electoral and parliamentary system as a counterweight to the ossified nomenklatura control system of the Communist Party. But Gorbachev was such a creature and master of the latter that he had never been comfortable in the electoral or parliamentary arenas.

Could the future then simply bring a further transition from Gorbachev to some representative of the next generation like Anatoly Sobchak—with Yeltsin as a transitional figure who validated democracy for ordinary Russians but who was not of the generation capable of creating new democratic institutions? Sobchak, the dynamic young mayor of newly renamed St. Petersburg, represented the best in the westward-looking perspectives of that legendary city. He was a cultured law professor who had joined the Communist Party only in 1988, when elections and the rule of law became part of its program. Sobchak had been with Yeltsin at the dacha in the morning of August 19 and had rushed back to take impressive command of his city. He dissuaded the military there from supporting the coup and organized the largest mass demonstration against it anywhere in the USSR on August 20.[43]

I thought about the way the old Russian wooden doll containing other dolls, the *matroshka*, had been politicized in the last year or so. I assumed that the sets then selling on the Arbat showing a Gorbachev outside a Brezhnev and a Stalin would soon be showing a Yeltsin outside Gorbachev, and wondered then if there might subsequently be a Sobchak outside Yeltsin.

The image of the *matroshka* had long been a favorite of mine for discussing Russia. It was suggested by Churchill's famous remark of October 1939 about Russia being "a riddle wrapped in a mystery inside an enigma." It had always seemed to me that the split and layered nature of Russian reality operated as much within individuals as between them, as much between generations as between leaders. I had from the beginning seen Gorbachev himself as something of a *matroshka*: a westward-looking face underneath a hard, Leninist exterior. In 1978, during the last surge of imperial repression under Brezhnev, I argued that "there is a second layer already visible behind the outer face of increased military power." The face on that doll showed "the weary expression of a human energy crisis," but underneath that layer lay a third doll with the more animated face of an altogether new generation of leaders. These, I suggested, might challenge "the very ideology of the Soviet system itself" by introducing administrative decentralization, the incentive principle, an accommodation with religion, and a real legislature.[44]

I had not foreseen then that these changes would be so long in coming and yet so sudden in arriving as they proved to be. But, of course, until very recently few people believed that fundamental change would come at all in the Soviet system, and those were generally the small minority who considered the Soviet system not that bad to begin with and perpetually deserving of a more accommodating Western attitude. My view had always been that there was deep inner strength in Russia but that inner forces could never transform Russia so long as its external force was successfully sustaining the imperial identity that legitimized the Leninist political machine.

What was new now was that the Leninist political machine was no longer able to sustain economically its external power—and no longer able to hold back actuarially the arrival of a new generation with a background totally different from that of any post-Stalinist leader prior to Gorbachev. The face of the new generation that I now saw on the Soviet *matroshka* was less that of Gorbachev or even Yeltsin than a composite of the restive younger generation that had grown up during the period of stagnation under Brezhnev.

In updating my talk on "Russia in Search of Itself" for delivery in Moscow a week before the coup, I suggested that this younger generation was in the process of introducing one of those tempestuous, sudden changes in its total culture (I used the term *vzryv*: explosion) that Russians tend to create after long periods of silence. It produced the explosion faster and more dramatically than I had expected. They clearly wanted something more than a repetition of the Khrushchev concept of reformed Communism. But would they ultimately, perhaps inadvertently, contribute to the frustration of reform as the younger radicals had under Gorbachev's model, Alexander II?

The young "nihilists" of the 1860s had preached an intolerant scientism that laid the basis for Lenin's revolutionary absolutism. Young Russians of the late 1980s were, on the contrary, in rebellion against Marxist materialism and its totalitarian political offspring. Their generation was deeply repelled by the inhuman consequences of central-ized control under a pseudo-scientific doctrine.

Having declared freedom from its Communist past, young Russia wondered how to use freedom to build a better future. Already during those exciting days in August, Russians were beginning to draw on three great and previ-ously neglected sources of strength: the experience of the West, the energy of the East, and their own memory. With the totalitarian fever broken, those three elements all seemed essential for the recovery. They suggested that a full and lasting transformation of Russia might indeed really be possible. Whatever their prospects and timetable might be in the future, those three forces gave reason for hope, be-cause the rich potentials of Western institutions, Siberian resources, and the Russian spiritual heritage are not likely soon to be exhausted. It is to an examination of each of these elements that we turn now in trying to see how break-ing old power involved animating new forces during the August crisis.

PART FOUR

Forces of Renewal

8

Waves from the West

The first element in transforming the consciousness of a new Russian generation was the influence of the West. New means of communication brought word from without, which strangely and unexpectedly seemed to harmonize with the voice from within. An awakened conscience required conscionable institutions, and burgeoning new means of electronic interconnection accelerated the rhythm and pace of change.

Just as the railroad and the telegraph opened up Russia in irreversible ways in the 1860s and 1870s, so the jet plane and the new electronic world of television and telefax was preparing Russia inexorably for change in the 1970s and 1980s. It was not just a question of East German access to West German or Baltic access to Scandinavian television; there had been continuing broadcasts from the West and a gradual seepage of Western ideas through increased travel into the Soviet establishment and eventually directly into Soviet television.

Although until very recently foreign travel had been largely confined to the nomenklatura itself, growing exposure to the West had its effect on the Russian establishment, particularly in an area not generally thought to have political consequences: individual academic exchanges.

I first become aware of such a possibility through the late Rem Khokhlov, the former rector of Moscow University, who died a few years ago heroically trying to rescue a friend from a mountain-climbing accident. He was one of the USSR's most gifted laser scientists and could have become just another cog in the military–industrial complex. But a year on academic exchange at Stanford had exposed him to more than physics; and this remarkable man introduced the first teaching of American studies into Moscow University and devised a plan in the mid-1970s (finally now being put into effect) to introduce similar courses more broadly throughout the USSR. I thought of him at the time of the summit meetings in Moscow in June 1988, when President Reagan made a speech at Moscow University (to which I had made some small contribution) and presented the university with the microfilmed versions of the papers of Washington, Jefferson, and Lincoln from the Library of Congress.

Alexander Yakovlev, perhaps the closest adviser to Gorbachev in his early years, first learned about the possibilities of a free society during his year as an exchange student in Columbia University. He played a key role not only in explaining the West to the more sheltered Gorbachev but also in criticizing Gorbachev's later conservative drift and in rallying to Yeltsin's support during the coup.

The extraordinary multiplier effects of one person's deep exposure can be illustrated by the case of a young political scientist named Vladimir Shtinov, whom I had gotten to know in 1990 on a visit to Sverdlovsk (now Ekaterinburg). Shtinov may have been the only person, up until the last year or so, ever to have come to America on an academic exchange from this center of military industry in the deep interior of Russia. On the basis of his year in Buffalo he has introduced at Sverdlovsk University some of the first serious studies of comparative politics and democratic political philosophy anywhere in Russia. Shtinov also served as a kind of foreign policy adviser to the reform-minded mayor of a city that is Yelstin's most loyal political base.

Commercial and managerial contacts with the West grew rapidly under Gorbachev and brought a new generation of Russian technicians into new kinds of contact with the West. The belated advent of computerization created offices with an international ambience and brought Russia, no less than the other republics, into an international network of instantaneous electronic communication that played a decisive role in the defeat of the putsch.

The Russian term for "on the air" (*v efir*) has—quite literally—an ethereal ring that is missing from the English equivalent. What goes into or through "the ether" is not, presumably, quite the same as what one finds on the ground in ordinary Soviet life. I thought of this the night before the putsch, when I appeared as the guest on a talk show for Echo Moscow. I was amazed at the detailed knowledge evident in questions called in from all over Russia. This remarkable radio operation reaches an audience in the tens of millions from two small, grungy rooms in a walk-up apartment near Red Square. It was shut down by the junta but reappeared twice in different places, along with Radio Russia and, of course, broadcasts from abroad: Radio Liberty, the Voice of America, Deutsche Welle, and the BBC. Thus, Gorbachev under house arrest in the Crimea got his news from broadcasts that he had once helped to jam; at his return press conference he mentioned first the BBC, widely celebrated at this time with the jingle:

Est obichai na rusi   There is a custom in Russia
nochiu slushat bi-bi-si.[45] At night to listen to BBC.

In the midst of the fearful uncertainties of those forty-eight crucial hours, one of its best chroniclers has written that information was quite simply "the most precious thing there is in all the world."[46] The human wall might not have held had it not come rapidly to depend on the local transmissions every two hours from "Radio White House," which were then tape-recorded and distributed to factories and schools all over Moscow. One of the characteristic images around the White House during that period was that of people clustering around transistor radios for the latest news. Inside the White House, the image was rather that of key leaders constantly on telephones gathering information and enlisting support all over Moscow. The deputy mayor of Moscow, Yuri Luzhkov, appears to have been a kind of anchor man on the telephone bank dealing with civilian Moscow; Vice President Rutskoi with high-ranking political figures; and General Kobets with the military sector. Telephone lines in the White House were only sporadically and imperfectly interdicted; reserve communications were brought in on standby ships in the Moscow River should they have been completely cut off.

And what was coming in "through the ether" was for the most part what was being sent out by fax, by E-mail, and by telephone from a variety of communication centers inside and outside the White House. Friendly forces within the television transmission center in Ostankino kept lines open for direct CNN television transmission from the White House, which was played back in many Moscow Hotels even though Soviet television was completely censored and the Ostankino Center totally surrounded by armored forces loyal to the junta.

The eighth entry to the Parliament building acquired a kind of reverential status, for that is where the Xerox machine stood. It reproduced the edicts and bulletins that the Russian government was continuously issuing. I remember repeated calls over the megaphone on the night of the nine-teenth for someone to repair a Xerox machine, run a new E-mail installation, etc. And because so many young professionals of the new information industry were among the defenders of the White House, someone was almost always available to perform the task. The information professionals were almost as important to the defense of the White House as the Afghan veterans.

Modern means of communication enabled the Yeltsin forces to conduct an extraordinarily effective psychological warfare campaign against the forces who were supposed to have been loyal to the junta. By instantly advertising every military defection to the White House, they encouraged others to follow and potential attackers to stall for time. Because they operated from one central headquarters, the forces in the White House soon came to control the information agenda, even though the junta controlled the centers of information. The junta was widely scattered and only sporadically gave clear directions to the media. It did not even have an official television spokesman, let alone one capable of inspiring fear and respect. Its one official appearance was at a press conference, where the members looked ill at ease and not altogether unified. I remember watching it on television with some depressed Russian friends late on that first day, when it looked to many as if the putsch were a *fait accompli.* One bright young Russian university student punctured the gloom by saying simply, "They look like the defendants at Nuremberg."

Of course, Russia was energized to break out of its totalitarian cocoon not just by instantaneous new forms of communication but also by a few central ideas from the West that almost everyone was increasingly capable of absorbing: the importance of a rule of law to check arbitrary power, of popular elections to ensure choice, and of local rights and a nongovernmental civil society to solve problems close to

103

the source and without the intrusion of a central bureau-cratic state. Gorbachev's partial moves in each of those directions had led to a desire to go faster in each; the grow-ing opportunity to travel to and talk with the West acceler-ated the interest in democratizing reforms.

It was the ideal of an open, democratic society—not of a more open, market economy—that brought young Russia to the barricades.[47] Even though many of those on the barricades were young entrepreneurs involved in the fledg-ling private sector economy, they knew that the junta was probably no less likely than the Russian Republic govern-ment to open up the economy. Indeed, it was widely be-lieved that the junta was planning an option similar to what they conceived to be Chile's system under Pinochet or South Korea's: a combination of military repression politi-cally with an openness to international investment and pri-vate sector initiative economically.

I had seen, among the five hundred or so Russians who have come to use the Library of Congress during the past two years, how intense their interest in the institutions of democracy is. But the putsch period made it even clearer to me how specially important the United States is as a distinct object of study and hoped-for partner within the more gen-eral category of "the West." The Russian discovery of Amer-ica in this quincentennial time of Columbus's voyage of discovery operates at four levels.

First and most universal is a fascination with the spon-taneity and directness of American mass culture, which has conquered Russia even more than it has many Western countries. The rock music, the slogans on T-shirts and buttons, the world of jeans, guitars, and jogging clothes—all have grown continuously in popularity under glasnost and were particularly in evidence around the White House.

Second and more important has been the recent impact on an essentially conservative Russian society of the more conservative side of America's political and cultural spectrum. I may be predisposed to stress this, having accompanied President and Mrs. Reagan to the Moscow summit in June 1988. But I genuinely believe that his firm early demonstration of political and military strength and proof that an American President could get reelected without first going to a summit was indispensable in causing the Communist leaders to undertake a genuine change of course. Then, in his second term, Reagan was able to make movement toward democratization, in effect, the price of a series of summits that legitimated Gorbachev internationally. Reagan combined personal friendship with Gorbachev and a continued affirmation directly to the Russian people of both the religious roots and the economic benefits of democracy. The very qualities that annoyed many of President Reagan's critics at home—the simplicity of his message and use of moralistic language ("evil empire")—found a certain resonance among Russians, who were beginning to cut loose from the sophisticated rationalizations in which Gorbachev was still trying to wrap his reform Communism.

I remember watching Gorbachev's first report on the Reykjavik mini-summit come on the television set in a bar in Odessa in October 1986. After only a few sentences, the eminently ordinary Russian crowd switched off the television set (just as the crowd in Dzerzhinsky Square was to turn off his broadcast). When I asked my neighbor why he didn't want to hear more about this fateful meeting, he replied: "We only want the answers to two questions: Will there be war? and Will there be more food on the table? You can tell from the expression on his face and the tone of his voice that the answer to both is no; so why listen to all the crap?"

It was evident then—and supported by my informal poll of taxi drivers in August 1991—that Reagan was more popular than Gorbachev among Russians and perhaps second only to Margaret Thatcher (revered as *zheleznaia ledi*: the iron lady) in overall popularity among world political leaders. Reagan seemed to have some of the directness and inner core of values that also made Yeltsin instinctively popular with ordinary Russians. A similarly warm feeling developed toward President Bush, particularly after he moved from his more cautious initial reaction to the coup into becoming the first foreign leader to telephone Yeltsin and publicly support the resistance.

There had been strong links since President Carter between liberal America and the human rights movement in Russia. But the growing activity of culturally conservative groups from America within Russia gave a new dimension to the democratic movement that enabled it to play better in the Russian version of Peoria or Dubuque. Evangelical and Pentecostal Christians were renting stadiums for revivals and warning against any tendency to make the Orthodox Church a state religion. The conservative political organizer Paul Weyrich was conducting seminars all over the Russian heartland on grassroots electoral campaigning for the democratic movement.

A third level of the Russian interest in America lies in the psychological and cultural fascination Russians have always had with their principal Western adversary. Russia does not have a securely self-confident culture like England or China. It has always had a tendency to borrow culturally from whomever it was opposing politically. The Russians took their art and religion from Byzantium in the tenth century and their first modern governmental institutions from the Swedes in the eighteenth, though only after fighting each for many decades. The United States in the late twentieth century replaced the Germany of the late nineteenth and early twentieth centuries (and the France of the late eighteenth and early nineteenth centuries) as the essential "West" that Russians must both publicly confront and privately learn from.

Since it had been a Cold War rather than a hot one, and since the floodgates of communication were more open than in any past era, there was greater willingness than ever before to learn directly and openly from this new protagonist/model. And there was a new reason for doing so. A new, educated generation realized that, simply as a practical matter, America was the most relevant case study for their new task of building a democracy in a multiethnic, rapidly industrialized, continentwide civilization with a healthy civil society and private sector economy.

In almost every area of ferment in the USSR there is the desire for an American counterpart contact—not just because we have so long been the other scorpion in the superpower bottle, but because there are roughly comparable human needs and many common problems that smaller or more homogeneous countries do not have. The new constitution that was completed for the Russian Republic under the commission headed by Oleg Rumiantsev called for the separation of powers, the proclamation of rights, and the federal layering of authority in a representative republic. This democratic constitution was not immediately adopted after its unveiling in the fall of 1991 because of the perceived need to concentrate first on pressing economic problems. But it was largely American in its inspiration, and even some of the criticism focused on American alternatives: a preference in the overcentralized Russian context for the even greater limitations put on central power by the Articles of Confederation, which predated the Constitution.

I felt some modest satisfaction in the work the Library of Congress was doing to help Russians, like other East Europeans, build the information infrastructure for a more open and democratic society. By the end of 1991 the Library of Congress was helping the Leningrad Academy of Sciences Library recover from its disastrous fire, advising the new Russian Archival Ministry on opening up the long-closed archives of the Communist Party, conducting a weeklong joint conference with the troubled Lenin Library in Moscow, and exploring the possibility of helping both the all-union and the Russian parliaments build small approximations of our Congressional Research Service. Congress itself was exploring the latter activity as part of a series of efforts to support parliament-building in Eastern Europe under an imaginative commission headed by Martin Frost.

That the U.S. Congress's efforts may well have been the most extensive form of technical aid provided by any American institution seemed a somewhat disturbing fact. I had written shortly after my return about the need to bring far larger numbers of the new Russian generation and its leadership over to America and to establish more institution-to-institution exchanges with the emerging new institutions of democratic governance and the civil society. But there seemed to be many political pressures opposed to having elected officials champion a major new national effort overseas when they might be accused of neglecting problems at home in an election year. Thus the expectations raised by August of greatly increased opportunities for exposure to American institutions and processes seemed somewhat deflated subsequently. I was left with the fear that the heights of hope might give way to depths of disillusionment. Out of this might well come some fascist-type movement feeding on the hardships of the transition, a movement able to make the United States once again the external enemy "in part because at a crucial breakpoint in history, we were unwilling to give more of ourselves to help others practice the ideals we had so long been preaching."[48]

However important Western and American models might

be for the process of change in Russia, they still arrived largely "through the ether" and were not as determinative on either the events of August or the prospects for the Russian future as those deeper native influences that came from both the breadth of their country (the awakening provinces exemplified by Sverdlovsk/Ekaterinburg) and the depth of their traditions (a resurgent Orthodox Church).

9

The Breadth of Russia

In my own quest for the sources of a post-Communist Russian identity, I had gone increasingly to the Russian provinces in recent years. Two visits in particular—to Archangel in the North in 1987 and Irkutsk in the East in 1990—seemed to confirm a suspicion that the outlying regions of Russia were bastions of authoritarian rule and conservative resistance to change.

In Arctic Archangel, I had been dazzled by the enormous scale models of long-since destroyed churches and monasteries in the Russian north built by the octogenarian S. P. Kalashnikov, only to find him reminiscing happily about his boyhood as a young Communist who had helped destroy many of the same churches.[49] My sense that there was something perversely reactionary about the provinces was deepened on a visit to the local Communist Party boss, who with great ceremony served me a dish of strawberries. He lingered over them with a kind of sensuous delight as if to revel in the fact that through some mysterious power of his own he was able to produce succulent fruit even amid the general poverty of the frozen north.

Equally unsettling had been my visit together with my son Tom to the Siberian city of Irkutsk in 1990. We were treated to real hospitality for a two-day journey around Lake Baikal with a delightful company of local political and cultural figures. But the lion of the group was also the most darkly reactionary in his political thinking: the writer Valentin Rasputin, who has supported almost every appeal for more social discipline in recent years. I had admired the early writings of this leader of the so-called village writers, but he seemed to put forward his combination of monarcho-clerical and antimodernist ecological ideas more to stop than to start discussion. He was not easy to talk to and conveyed little of the warmth or "broad Russian nature" I had hoped, perhaps naïvely, to find in him while surrounded by the relatively unspoiled beauty of his beloved Lake Baikal.

Those more expansive qualities I had met in Moscow during a long interview with a television group from another Siberian city, Krasnoiarsk, before setting off on my Siberian visit just a year before the coup attempt. And I had my eyes opened to an altogether different Siberia when I went to the city of Sverdlovsk shortly after it was opened to foreigners.

Sverdlovsk was Yeltsin's original political base; a core of old associates from there remained closest to Yeltsin throughout his ordeal in the White House. In his outer circle of defenders on the barricades was also a surprisingly large number of political activists and journalists from that same West Siberian city, many of whom had come to Moscow to attend the Congress of Compatriots. Sverdlovsk produced a public demonstration of 100,000, probably the largest in support of the resistance to the putsch for any location in the deep Russian interior. It was to a bunker 10-15 meters underground and 60 kilometers south of Sverdlovsk that Yeltsin secretly sent his deputy prime minister

111

and fellow Sverdlovian Oleg Lobanov and twenty-four others from Moscow during the first night of the putsch.[50] There they were to form the legal successor government of the Russian Republic in case Yeltsin and the others in the White House were killed or captured. From there on the second day of the putsch a telex link was set up with fifty-eight oblasts (provinces) and regions, most of which would otherwise have had little access to two-way communication with the Yeltsin forces.

It is strangely symbolic that *Sverdlovchane* (Sverdlovians) should be leading the resistance to an illegal putsch and that their distant city on the dividing line between Europe and Asia should be the potential locus of legitimacy for an alternative government. For in this same city the last Tsar, Nicholas II, had been exiled with all his family, and then murdered by Bolshevik putschists exactly seventy-three years and one month before this last Bolshevik putsch was launched. The same fate would have probably befallen this new source of alternate authority if this last Bolshevik junta had been as successful as the first in consolidating power in the distant European capital of the Russian empire. But this time Sverdlovsk, like all of Siberia, was no longer the place that received rejected exiles from the authoritarian center. It was sending to that center elected radical democrats from a resurgent periphery.

"You must understand. We never had serfdom here," Rudolf Pikhoya, the head of the history department at the Ural State University, had explained to me as we sweated together in a rural sauna outside Sverdlovsk just a year before the putsch. A certain freedom from, and defiance of, "the center" was clearly a part of the mentality of Russians in Siberia no less than of minority nationalities in the Russian empire. At a time when Gorbachev was involved in his usual indecisive economic discussions in Moscow and in telephone talks with foreign leaders, Yeltsin was using the summer months of 1990 for an exhausting speaking tour of Siberia. "He is listening to as well as talking with people—and in places no other Soviet leader has ever even visited," another Sverdlovsk official explained.

From that first hot bath just off the plane with Pikhoya through a nonstop series of meetings with the political and cultural leaders of the city, I became caught up in August 1990 with a spirit of independence and hopefulness that contrasted with the fatalism and apocalypticism so prevalent in Moscow and St. Petersburg. Within this grim-looking center of large-scale production for the military–industrial complex of the USSR an amazing political and cultural revival was clearly occurring unnoticed by almost anyone in the West, or even in Moscow.

A lively exhibit of Jewish culture was being held in the main public park of the city, complete with impromptu lectures by visiting rabbis and the public sale of the *Jerusalem Post* to a large cluster of interested readers. When I asked one of the city officials why they had decided to have this major event in a city with only a tiny Jewish population, he replied that the Jewish heritage was an important part of broader Russian culture and added that "we must have something to learn from the Jews if all the reactionaries in Moscow are so opposed to them."

Some in Moscow, to be sure, had been dazzled by the Sverdlovsk opera company's new productions of traditional Russian operas at the Bolshoi the previous autumn, and many admired Sverdlovsk's new composer, Vladimir Kobeikin, and its rock group Notilius-Pompilius. But no one had warned me that Sverdlovsk was at the forefront not just of the most immaterial of the arts—music—but of the most concrete and political form of artistic expression: the propagandistic exhibition.

The permanent exhibit of Soviet history in the Sverdlovsk

Museum of the Young Communist League introduced me to a genuinely new Russian consciousness. At the entrance were two rooms perfectly preserved from the Stalin era to remind people of the propagandistic past. They looked not unlike most rooms in most Soviet museums up until the putsch. One then passed through a tunnel into a new world that represented a devastating critique of the entire Soviet experiment presented in an altogether understated and therefore doubly powerful way. There was a vast map of the Sverdlovsk oblast, a region about the size of New Jersey, showing the ninety-odd prison camps located there and a necrology of famous people who had died in each. There were sections documenting the horrors of the Civil War and forced industrialization as well as a particularly moving wall of letters written from Afghanistan by soldiers from the Sverdlovsk area recording their sorrow and anger over their mission.

Near the exit of the museum was a place for subscribing to a wide range of reform journals and publications of the Ural and Siberian region manned by a quiet, clean-cut team of young people. These were not the usual unkempt youthful radicals, but an almost reverential group who respectfully offered me and other departing visitors material on the museum and the democratic movement, rather the way acolytes in the Orthodox church offered worshipers candles to take out into the darkness on the great feast of the Epiphany in January.

I had known that Sverdlovsk was Yeltsin country but wanted to meet members of the reactionary old guard as well, knowing that they still presided over the great plants that built the missiles and had helped produce the ecological disasters of the recent past. So before going there, I had asked Yeltsin's conservative rival, Prime Minister Nikolai Ryzhkov, who had been an industrial leader in Sverdlovsk, to suggest friends of his with whom I could talk. Only when they too proved to have become mostly Yeltsin sympathizers did I realize the depth of disaffection with the center. Only when I began probing into the origins of the unusual family name of Ryzhkov's principal friend in Sverdlovsk—Eduard Rossel (Russell)—did I begin to guess the secret source of the moral force I was finding in this unlikely industrial metropolis.

Many in Sverdlovsk had non-Russian names or lineage, largely because so many creative people had been exiled there and because this city was as far west as many former Siberian prisoners were allowed to return. Seeds of freedom were planted here by forcibly exiled national minorities and foreign captives, as well as by the productive and entrepreneurial peasants whom Stalin called kulaks and tried to eliminate as a class during collectivization. He succeeded in silencing all these creative elements for a long period and in killing off an entire generation. But some of them survived, married local Russian girls, and produced children who were coming back to haunt the repressive imperial system that Stalin had left behind.

It had been easier for Yeltsin to denounce that system when he came from Sverdlovsk to head the Moscow party organization, than to define a clear democratic alternative. But it also rapidly became clear to Muscovites that Yeltsin's contempt for the "partocracy" was not simply a matter of populist demagoguery, but of deeper moral revulsion. He began visiting ordinary people and renouncing many of the traditional perquisites of a Politburo leader. Gennady Burbulis, Yeltsin's closest associate from Sverdlovsk who became his deputy prime minister, has suggested that Yeltsin's conflict with Gorbachev was rooted in the latter's consistent failure to establish "a deeply moral relationship with the people of his city."

Burbulis may have helped Yeltsin link his moral passion with the unfamiliar institutions of political and economic freedom when he hit upon what he described as the basic "formula" for their democratic program for Russia during an electoral debate in Sverdlovsk. His opponent was Arnold Epp, another Sverdlovian of partly foreign origin who professed to be equally interested in reform, but as the privileged head of a construction institute was stressing the need for more productivity rather than the need for greater freedom that Burbulis had emphasized. A listener jolted Burbulis when he summarized the difference by saying: "If you want to live better, vote for Epp. If you want to be freer, for Burbulis." He realized then that this was a false dichotomy, and that "in order to live better, we have to become freer."[51]

I felt the force of this determination to be freer in order to live better—both materially and morally—with every chance contact I had with friends from Sverdlovsk in Moscow during the period of troubles. I met V. P. Bykodorov, the slight, soft-spoken director of the Sverdlovsk Museum, in the Church of the Assumption inside the Kremlin on the morning of the coup. He was there full of hope to film what he claimed would be a "historical event": the opening of the doors onto the great square so that the Patriarch could address the people there for the first time publicly since the Bolshevik Revolution. Other members of the large film crew from Sverdlovsk later in the day expressed disappointment to me that there had not been a clear message disavowing the putsch. But they, like others from the deep interior who had come to record the Congress of Compatriots' rediscovery of Russia, were by then preoccupied with what they could do to help defend the White House.

The night after the danger had passed, one of the young Sverdlovians came to my room late at night to remind me of our brief meeting in the museum a year before and to tell me that it was his thirty-third birthday. When he spoke excitedly of the democratic victory and of the fact that it had been achieved on the day when he reached the age of Christ at the time of His crucifixion, I asked if he were a believer. He said that he and most of his generation were not, but were deeply curious about this lost part of their heritage and hopeful that Christianity would play a renewed role in the new society that lay ahead.

A few days later, as I was preparing to leave, a call came from Pikhoya, the historian-host who had introduced me to the rural baths in Sverdlovsk a year earlier and had shown me the great collection of old Russian religious books that young people from Sverdlovsk had gathered from outlying Old Believer communities in the Urals and Western Siberia. He apologized for not seeing me off. He was now installed almost permanently in the former headquarters of the Communist Party Central Committee and was in charge of preserving and opening up the entire historical record of the Party. Yeltsin had brought Pikhoya from Sverdlovsk earlier in the summer to head the archives of the Russian Republic. After the coup collapsed, Pikhoya led a posse from the White House to the former Communist Party Headquarters on Old Square near the Kremlin on August 23, when he heard that former members of the now defunct Party were destroying or carting off much of their own historical record.

Pikhoya and his wife, Ludmilla, one of Yeltsin's key speechwriters, had been with Yeltsin at his dacha and for all three days at the White House, around the clock. Both his father and his grandfather had perished for political reasons in Siberia, and the Pikhoyas had quietly resolved that they were willing to die so that their own son could at last live in freedom. As I got to know him better on three subsequent trips to Moscow after the putsch, I recognized in this short, stocky figure something of both the broad horizons and the rock-hard toughness of his native Siberia. A Russian Mr. Smith had come to the Russian Washington. He was determined to take the 75,000,000 items in the immense archives of the Communist Party Central Committee out of the hands of the few politicians who had used them in secret to perpetuate their own power. He would prepare them for open use by all the world's historians in order to get at the truth of the totalitarian nightmare.

Hope continued to predominate among the *Sverdlovchane*—just as it had brought them together instinctively and immediately in those early hours of the coup, when most of Moscow was still paralyzed by fear. The essence of the great change of August was the replacement of the politics of fear by the politics of hope: the migration of the ultimate source of authority from the threat of a cell in the Lubyanka to the promise of a frontier beyond Sverdlovsk. For beyond all the rusting and pollution-bearing industrial plants of that city lay the untapped natural resources of Siberia, beginning with the immense Tyumen oil and gas fields just to the east. The underused human resources seemed equally great. A public opinion poll conducted on August 20, the second day of the coup, showed far more opposition in Krasnoiarsk, a city nearly as large as Sverdlovsk and 2,000 kilometers deeper into Siberia, than in any of the three other cities surveyed in European Russia and the Ukraine. More than three-fourths of the population of that distant industrial city considered the putsch illegal and likely to worsen their economic conditions.[52]

The mayor of Sverdlovsk, Yury Samarin, a former naval captain, told me in August 1990 that the natural wealth of Western Siberia could potentially be delivered by ship to the West through a series of canals and rivers that led into the Black and Mediterranean seas. Like other Siberians, he was seeking economic as well as political links with the West. He explained to me that Yeltsin inspired hope because, during his rule in Sverdlovsk, he never promised anything he did not deliver. In contrast to traditional Communist rhetoric that promised a coming utopia, Yeltsin spoke only of small, concrete benefits. But he always delivered, unlike Gorbachev, who only talked about delivering.

The very strength of the ferment in Sverdlovsk produced a local reactionary group anxious to preserve the vanishing Communist power by revalidating the politics of fear. A small protofascist nationalist group, "The Fatherland," arose in the course of 1990. Aleksandr Tiziakov, the *de facto* leader of military–industrial production in the USSR and a longtime veteran of the giant Kalinin machine-building factory of Sverdlovsk, was one of the coup leaders.[53] But the former head of Tiziakov's party organization, Aleksandr Volkov, had become a reform-minded deputy to the Supreme Soviet of the USSR in Moscow and, like almost all active younger politicians in Siberia, opposed the putsch.

In the course of a long talk with Burbulis in November 1991, I came to realize that these ostensibly parochial Siberians from the deep interior actually had a richer sense of Russia's interrelationships with other countries than do many of their more experienced but jaded contemporaries in Moscow and Leningrad. Like his friend Pikhoya in the archives, Burbulis in the White House saw Russia's Communist past as a global and not merely a Russian problem. Without asking for help or engaging in self-pity, he suggested that Russia had saved the rest of Europe immense suffering by becoming the testing ground that humanity had to find somewhere for the utopian revolutionary infatuations that were everywhere prevalent at the time. The clear implication was that Russia was now the testing ground for something radically different—equally innovative and equally global in its implications, but far more hopeful than the totalitarian past.

Not long after the coup, Sverdlovsk was renamed Ekaterinburg, discarding its association with Yakov Sverdlov, an early Bolshevik implicated in the murder of the last Tsar's family, and resuming its original name honoring an illustrious earlier Tsarina, Catherine the Great. The large statue of Sverdlov in Moscow was one of the relatively few in the capital to be destroyed along with that of Dzerzhinsky.

Reflecting on my brief but inspiring links with this city that was returned to Catherine after Leningrad was returned to Peter, I realized that its greatest secret lay not in where the Tsar's family or the gulags' victims were buried in the past, but in how hope had been rekindled among its young people in the present. The direct manner of speech used by Yeltsin and his associates, which Moscow cab drivers described as *priamoi* (direct) and *muzhitsky* (manly), seemed during those heady August days to have purified the Russian language of both Communist jargon and parliamentary verbosity. As I talked with some of the proud yet modest Siberians on the barricades, the glimmer of hope that Pasternak put at the end of *Doctor Zhivago* came back to me.

With Zhivago dead and all of Russia ravaged by Stalin's purges and war's horrors, Pasternak gave us a final glimpse of a laundry girl, Tanya, whom we are led to think may be in some sense Zhivago's progeny who has survived it all and come back to Moscow from "somewhere in the depths of Russia where the language is still pure."[54] At the very end of the prose part of the novel, the lonely poet seemed to have foreseen, even amid the revived repression of the late Khrushchev years, what most social scientists have not been able to imagine since: that "the depths of Russia" might transform Moscow, and that an unexpected future might move "tangibly into the streets," filling those there with "the unheard music of happiness that flowed all about them and into the distance."

Although victory had not brought the relief and freedom that were expected at the end of the war, nevertheless portents of freedom filled the air throughout the postwar period, and they alone defined its historical significance.[55]

10

The Depth of Rus

Chudo, "a miracle," was the word almost everyone used in Moscow that August to describe how it all ended so much sooner and better than anyone had expected or could believe. The favorite professor of one of the largest student contingents on the barricades (Vladislav Kovalev of the Journalism Faculty of Moscow University) used to define a miracle as what occurs "when you overcome the weight of what you are accustomed to."[56] The professor died at the very time of the coup, and did not live to see his students help cast off the weight of fear that Moscow had so long become accustomed to. How they were able to do so seemed to many a miracle in a much more mysterious—and ultimately religious—sense.

For the last few years, with rising intensity, the air in Moscow has been charged with otherwordly foreboding. The death of a secular materialism promising utopia had opened the way for rediscovering the supernatural and a thirst for prophecy. Already by the late 1980s the clairvoyant charlatan purveyor of supersensory healing Anatoly Kashpirovsky was the most popular television personality

122

in Russia; the Hare Krishnas were enjoying a certain vogue; and the apocalyptical *He Who Did Not Return* had become perhaps the most popular new piece of fiction writing with its depiction of Moscow in terminal disintegration by 1993.[57]

In their search for a vocabulary to express this rediscovered spiritual dimension of life, the Russians drifted inexorably back to the half-forgotten, much distorted heritage of the Russian Orthodox Church. For decades there had been a slow out-migration of persecuted Christians from the politically docile Orthodox Church, with its mysterious liturgy, to the ever growing Baptist Church and, increasingly, to the Pentecostals. But now there was a kind of in-migration of Russian Orthodoxy into the Russian consciousness—even of the Communist establishment itself. The celebration of the Millennium of Christianity in Russia during 1988 had involuntarily been transformed into a kind of Russian national festival. Gorbachev had invited the Orthodox hierarchy into the Kremlin for the first public meeting with a Communist leader since Stalin had done the same during the war in 1943. Raisa Gorbachev had appeared on the stage of the Bolshoi Theater along with the Stalinist head of government, Andrei Gromyko, at a bizarre, quasi-religious state ceremony ending with the ringing of bells newly hung in the ceiling of the theater. I remember even Gromyko's wife flying in Air Force 1 from Leningrad to Moscow in June 1988 and explaining to Nancy Reagan, the great Christian scholar Dmitry Likhachev, and me with great solemnity that she had concluded that there was indeed some kind of supreme being in the universe.

The thirst for prophecy found a popular subject and new links with Orthodox tradition early in 1991, when the rediscovered remains of Saint Seraphim of Sarov were brought back to Moscow in February from their long incarceration

in the Leningrad Museum of Atheism. Seraphim, prototype of the monastic elders who counseled lay people and
were celebrated in Dostoevsky's *Brothers Karamazov*, had
predicted that Russia would renounce its faith and go
through great suffering but would in the end return to Orthodoxy. With church properties being given back to believers and a general religious revival well under way, that
prophecy seemed on the way to being vindicated by the
time Seraphim's remains were moved with great festivity
from Moscow to their historic and final resting place in the
rural cloister of Diveevo in early August 1991.

Especially important to the faithful was the consecration
on August 16 of the oldest church in the Russian republic,
the Cathedral of Santa Sophia in historic Novgorod. Standing next to Patriarch Alexis II at the ceremony was the vice
president of the Russian Republic and future hero of the
defense of the White House during the putsch, Aleksandr
Rutskoi. When the sun suddenly came out and lit up in
splendor the newly gilded onion domes, Rutskoi confided
that he was experiencing a miracle for the second time in
his life. The first miracle had been a vision of the Mother
of God that had come to him as an air force officer in
Afghanistan when he was preparing to pick up a grenade to
kill himself rather than risk the shame of capture. Somewhere from the Orthodox past faith had returned on that
occasion to this much decorated Hero of the Soviet Union,
who played a key role in establishing contact with the Patriarch and bringing the leader of the Church into open
support for the resistance.

About 10 A.M. on Sunday morning, August 18—precisely when the KGB was ordered on alert as the first act of
the coup—Patriarch Alexis was beginning another in his
unending series of services celebrating the formal return to
the Church of another historic house of worship. This time
it was the main cathedral of the Monastery of Our Lady of

the Don in Moscow, where the most revered and uncom-
promisingly anti-Communist Patriarch of the modern era,
the imprisoned Patriarch Tikhon, had been buried in
1925.[58] The way out of the long bondage of the Church
under Tikhon's successors began for Alexis exactly twenty-
four hours later, on the first morning of the coup, when,
precisely at the time large-scale tank units began moving
into Red Square, the Patriarch was beginning a liturgy for
the Feast of the Transfiguration in the Cathedral of the
Assumption within the Kremlin.

Just as Pasternak in *Doctor Zhivago* interweaves his fic-
tional account of the Revolution of 1917 with the signs and
symbols of Holy Week, so the real-life events of the democratic revolution of 1991 seem to have been interlinked
with—and framed by—the feasts of the Transfiguration and
the Assumption. The entire fever break with totalitarianism
was both opened and closed with festal Patriarchal liturgies:
for the Transfiguration on the nineteenth and for the Assumption on the twenty-eighth. Both were held in the
Kremlin cathedral that was itself dedicated to the Assumption of the Virgin, the church in which the Tsars had traditionally been crowned and power legitimized before the
Bolshevik Revolution. In that same Cathedral of the Assumption on August 26 the Patriarch also held a requiem
for the three martyred boys from the barricades, which served
as the opening—and in a way the legitimating—event for
convening the democratic alternative to the putsch: the All-
Union Congress of Peoples' Deputies, which began its deliberations immediately afterward inside the Kremlin. The
anathema against fraternal bloodletting which the Patriarch
issued at 1:30 A.M. on August 21, just before the expected
storming of the White House, was in the form of an inter-
cessory prayer to the Virgin-Protectress of Russia during the
fast that leads up to the Feast of her Assumption, her final,
triumphal entry into Heaven.

But it was not evident on the first day of the putsch, the Feast of the Transfiguration, that the Russian Orthodox hierarchy would break with its long record of deference if not servility toward secular authority. Although the Patriarch was reportedly urged by leaders of the Christian Democratic movement to speak up about the coup just before the liturgy, he only substituted "people" for "government and armed forces" in the prayer of intercession for Russia. He said nothing at all about surrounding events in his outdoor speech afterward in the Kremlin square, even though the sound of tanks could be clearly heard at several points in his address.

My sense of gloom about the role that the Church leadership might play in the crisis was deepened later that day by a conversation with Metropolitan Pitirim before the opening meeting of the Congress of Compatriots. The elegantly white-bearded Pitirim, perhaps the most photogenic and worldly of all the leaders of the Russian Church, has been a frequent promoter of peace conferences and international boards where funds are gathered and disbursed for cultural purposes. He and two young staff figures accompanying him from two of his boards clearly felt uncomfortable in a gathering largely sympathetic to the Yeltsin resistance. In response to the lightest of questions he indicated strong sympathy for the putsch's determination to restore discipline and order and his contempt for "the democracy of empty shelves." As the meeting began, one emigré asked that the group rise to show its solidarity with Gorbachev and Yeltsin. Pitirim, flushed with anger, remained stonily seated and left with his frightened acolytes shortly thereafter. I was even more worried about the position of the Church when I later learned that two other metropolitans, Juvenaly and Cyril, both considered more liberal, were also present at the meeting and had also remained seated.[59]

Behind the scenes, however, something more positive

may have been happening. After his silence at the morning liturgy, the Patriarch had apparently huddled with Juvenaly and Cyril and had informed key Church organizations by fax of the position that they made more broadly public the following day: no support for any new government structure without both word from Gorbachev and juridical assent by the Supreme Soviet, and a call to the armed forces to avoid bloodshed. The Yeltsin forces were allegedly assured by the Patriarch of his support through Rutskoi by midafternoon of the nineteenth. The following night the Patriarch called on the armed forces to avoid fraternal bloodshed under pain of anathema in a theologically remarkable prayer broadcast to the troops threatening the White House just before their assault was expected:

Whoever takes up arms against his neighbor, against unarmed people, weighs down his soul with the heaviest of sins, cutting himself off from the Church and from God . . . may the Lord deliver us from the terrible sin of fratricide. . . . The Church does not and cannot bless an illegal, forcible, blood-letting action.[60]

The voice from on high would not have reached those below with authority had it not been for the dozen or so ordinary parish priests who had already joined with, and were ministering to, the unarmed human wall around the White House. First and foremost was Father Gleb Yakunin, a long-persecuted dissident priest who had become a popular member of the parliament of the Russian Republic and a thorn in the side of the reactionary elements in the hierarchy. Yakunin had blessed Boris Yeltsin at the previous darkest moment in his career, when he had left the Communist Party and seemingly all prospects for a future political career. Yakunin made a Hollywood-like escape into the metro from a team of security forces that came to arrest him on the morning of the coup and rushed over to become one of the most powerful speakers to the crowd around the White House. He faced down and brought to a halt one of the early advancing columns of tanks by standing in their path in full priestly regalia.[61]

Another activist priest, Father Aleksandr Borisov, delivered some 2,000 New Testaments to the tank troops who were threatening the White House and an equal number to its unarmed defenders. Other priests performed the purely pastoral function of praying with, baptizing, and counseling the miscellaneous defenders throughout the two dark and rainy nights when the outcome was still in doubt. Father Viacheslav Polosin, another elected deputy, played a key intermediary role with the Patriarch and later recalled how 250 militia men asked a priest to adminster confession and communion.

Thousands of young people, brought up in Bolshevism, confessed in chorus their faith in Christ the Savior in front of the White House while a priest blessed an icon of Him and placed it on the head tank alongside a three-colored Russian flag.[62]

Most of these barricade parishioners had never had any previous contact with the Church and might never again; but many were moved by the powerful epistle that the Patriarch then issued denouncing the coup as an "outrage against all that is holy in our Fatherland on the day when the Church celebrates the great feast of the Lord's Transfiguration." Russia had been saved, he suggested, by the Virgin-Protectress herself: "It was not my prayers, but the prayers of all of you that were heard and brought forth the miracle."[63]

Lay Christians no less than priests played a significant role. The altogether new Christian Democratic Party (a political party that had not existed in Tsarist Russia) guarded entryway 1A to the White House under icons of St. Seraphim and St. Nicholas—just as other groups staked out their own defensive point of honor. The head of that party, Viktor Aksiutich, was a key interlocutor with the commander of the Tamansky tank division, whose defection to the Yeltsin cause on the first night of the coup represented the first crack in the united front of military opposition to the Yeltsin camp.[64]

I remember standing in the rain outside the White House when the thrilling announcement that those attacking tanks had crossed over to defend the White House came over the loudspeakers. Amid the general chant of *mol-od-tsy* (good guys), there was a chilling realization that now some kind of armed confrontation was all but inevitable. "There will be bloodshed," one older woman quietly said to another, who answered by finishing the sentence almost in a whisper "as on the cross."

That thought came back to me several days later at the final farewell of the people of Moscow to the three boys who had died on the barricades. The leadoff speaker was the young disabled deputy Ilya Zaslavsky, one of the most uncompromising yet cheerful of democratic reformers. He was followed by Mayor Gavriil Popov, who imagined what very different things each of the young men might have given their country had they been able to live. It was as moving as the ending to one of the greatest of all war movies, *Ballad of a Soldier*, where a young soldier on leave bids a hurried farewell to his mother and the narrator tells us that he could have been so many things, but he was only a Russian soldier.

These fallen soldiers of August were repeatedly praised for having somehow earned for others the possibility of a fresh start by the purity and totality of their sacrifice. Their pictures were held high and floated like icons above the hundreds of thousands gathered in Manezh Square, where—a few days before on the first day of the putsch—only a few hundred had dared gather for the first demonstration. In praising the three young men, speakers often unconsciously invoked phrases and images used to describe the first of all Russian saints, Boris and Gleb. Those two youngest sons of the baptizer of Russia, Prince Vladimir, voluntarily accepted martyrdom in the hope of reuniting their divided people. The connection was not made explicitly, but never have I felt such a powerful sense of public identification with the Christian idea of the redemptive value of innocent suffering. Even Gorbachev, a professed atheist who up till then had shown no public recognition of sufferings other than his own during this period, choked up and lost his usual composure when he first mentioned the three boys in his brief remarks.

The emotional outpouring that accompanied the rally and procession through Moscow of the funeral cortege represented the only really large-scale participation of ordinary Muscovites in the events of August. The sense of empathy that one could sense everywhere with the idea that their innocent deaths had broader redemptive meaning arose out of not just the substratum of half-forgotten Christian belief but also recent efforts to extract some meaning from the sufferings of the Soviet era. As the full horror of the gulag system became known under the bright light of glasnost, many Russians have felt an intensified need to believe that innocent suffering served some kind of redemptive purpose. "My life ended when I entered Stalin's prisons, but *My Life* began," one old scholar told me in explaining his return to religion. He was using a Russian play on words between *zhizn* (life in its ordinary sense) and *zhitie* (used in holy writings to describe the experiences of saints and martyrs).

When free television returned after forty-eight hours of junta control, the resistance was instantly mythologized in a series of beautiful documentaries that portrayed the strug-

130

gle in the manner of the ancient chronicles—the original, Christian literature of Russia—as a pure struggle between good and evil, light and darkness. Moscow was again *belokamenny*, the "white-stoned" city of legend. Beauty as a spiritual quality and whiteness as the color of divinity seemed transposed from the figure of Christ on the classical icons of the Transfiguration into many of the figures and images that appeared on the newly liberated television screen: the whiteness of the White House, the haunting handsomeness of all three dead boys, the white hair of Yeltsin atop the tank, and the sudden appearance of the sun after forty-eight hours dominated by the dark nights and almost constant rain.

Most memorable of all for me in the continuous montage of television celebration was the statuesque dignity of eighty-four-year-old Dmitry Likhachev, a survivor of the first and in many ways most horrible of the gulags in Solovetsk, addressing a supporting rally of 250,000 from the Winter Palace with his message combining Christian nonviolence and democratic militance. St. Petersburg earned back its old name by standing firm with the Yelstin resistance from the beginning (its liberal mayor, Anatoly Sobchak, was at Yeltsin's dacha when the original resistance was formed) and produced the largest single public gathering in support of the resistance anywhere in Russia during the days of junta dominance.

Likhachev personifies both the Christian culture of Muscovy, which is his field of study, and the aristocratic culture of St. Petersburg, of which he may be the last living example. He has seen his own mission essentially in terms of Christian service ever since he was able to escape death because someone warned him he was on a list to be arrested one night during the purges of the late 1930s. He has seen his life as a kind of undeserved gift ever since and has felt a need to compensate somehow the unknown person who took his place in order to fill the necessary quota of victims. He felt a new sense of purpose in the 1980s after surviving a knife attack the night after he heroically cast his lonely vote in the Academy of Sciences against expelling Sakharov. He was saved on that occasion by a manuscript in his pocket which absorbed most of the blow, and in the age of glasnost he became a television tutor to the Russian nation on its forgotten Christian heritage as well as a champion of historical restoration. He also became an occasional counselor and guest of the Gorbachevs.

Likhachev had arranged the exhibit of Russian religious books from the most persecuted of all defenders of the traditional faith of Orthodoxy, the Old Believers, that was held at the Library of Congress during the June 1990 summit and was opened by Raisa Gorbachev. To see him rallying St. Petersburg back to democracy from the place where it had been overthrown in his youth (the Winter Palace headquarters of the provisional democratic government) was to see the illumination come alive from one of the chronicles—along with their basic message that long-suffering (*dolgoterpenie*) in the faith can bring unexpected gifts in miraculous ways.

The high point of the funeral procession in Moscow came when it passed the White House and Yeltsin addressed his unforgettable apology to the parents of the three boys: "Forgive me, your President, that I was not able to defend and save your sons." Forgiveness is what Russians ask of each other before they take communion, and what an earlier Boris had also asked of the Russian people with his dying breath in the greatest of all Russian operas, Mussorgsky's *Boris Godunov*. There was hardly a dry eye in Moscow. A new moral dimension was asserting itself in the leadership: Someone who was not responsible was accepting responsibility in a society where traditionally no one in power had accepted blame for much of anything.

Beyond accepting responsibility and asking forgiveness lay the deeper theological dimension of repentance. *Repentance* was the title of the most powerful movie to appear in the Gorbachev era, the great work of the Georgian film-maker Tengiz Abuladze, in which a dictator's destruction of a church becomes a central symbol.[65] The need for repentance became a central theme in the popular, if unofficial, side of the celebrations of the Millennium of Christianity in 1988. I remember being awakened at 3 A.M. in Moscow in May 1987 at an official church conference on the Millennium by a parish priest who simply wanted to tell me that the conference we were both attending had totally missed the overwhelming need for repentance—not just for its docility before the atheist state, but for its failure even to pray publicly for its own martyrs.

Crowds far larger than those that defended the White House rallied after the coup collapsed to witness the dismantling of the statue of the founder of the Soviet secret police, Feliks Dzerzhinsky, in front of KGB headquarters. What was remarkable about that gathering, and indeed the even larger crowds for the funerals, was their almost total lack of violence or even disorder. Moscow seemed to echo the "velvet" revolution in Prague in its realization that overcoming totalitarianism meant breaking with the enslaving passion for revenge that fed into the Communist culture of vengeance and scapegoatism. Only fourteen people were arrested, as the victorious forces of democracy seemed determined to end the totalitarian reign of institutionalized violence with an almost entirely nonviolent movement, looking to change within the individual rather than purges within the society as the driving force of real change.

This essentially nonviolent element derived from the sense of shared exhilaration that a new politics of hope had somehow triumphed over the old politics of fear. Old intractable divisions that hampered all previous Russian efforts at real reform seemed—at least for a time, at least in Moscow—to have been transcended. The conflict between the Slavophile and Westernizing tendencies seemed to be overcome in the determination of the surging crowds to move ahead more boldly both outward toward Western economic and political forms and inward toward older Russian beliefs and values. The classic tension between intellectuals and working people seemed to have been muted in the polyglot mixture of artists and writers with soldiers and workers around the White House.

Even the clouded past of Christian–Jewish relations seemed to enter a new phase in the funeral rites for the three boys. For the first time in Russian history an official state funeral included both the chanting of the Russian Orthodox "Eternal Memory" and a Reformed Jewish Kaddish. The one Jewish boy was laid to rest alongside the two Russians in an Orthodox cemetery that was to become an all-Russian place of pilgrimage.

It seems in retrospect fitting that there was a Jewish component to the two most moving moments of my last days there after the coup as a visiting Christian privileged to witness the rebirth of another Christian culture. First was the sudden unforgettable appearance of a smiling Mikhail Levner at a high point overlooking the entire reformist leadership of Russia as it assembled in a heavily guarded area behind the speakers' stand for the funeral of the three boys. This could have been the ideal sniper position the forces of the coup had long been looking for; how he talked his way in there I do not know to this day. But using the same ingenuity he has consistently shown in building up for us the best collection anywhere of Russian reformist literature, our man of the book in Moscow had scrambled up to a position that their men of war fortunately never reached. His smiling face looked down with the old buildings of Moscow University and its library in the background, somehow suggesting to me at that otherwise sad moment that sometimes, at least, books really do prevail over bullets.

I went directly from the funeral of the three boys in Moscow to spend my last weekend before returning to America in the newly restored monastery of Optina Pustyn, which had been the principal spiritual retreat for Gogol, Dostoevsky, and Tolstoy.[66] There one encountered little vignettes reminiscent of unfriendly Soviet caricatures of monastic life; monks ignorant about the events in Moscow, a visitor both hoarding in and spitting out food at the guest table, and monastic officials talking about raising funds for a bus to regulate the growing flow of visitors. But there was a restorative calm about it all—the most beautiful chanting I have ever heard at the evening service on Saturday and a sense of dynamism in the building of new agricultural enterprises and a new library by the sixty-five young monks who make up the community.

The surrounding countryside 150 miles south of Moscow has an almost English feel. The landscape is intimate and welcoming. The largely nineteenth-century buildings have a more human scale than the more majestic, older Russian monasteries to the north. Whereas the latter are often centered on giant cathedrals that transpose the wooden forms of a tent roof and onion dome into stone, the central building in Optina is the modest wooden Church of John the Baptist, which transposes the stone forms of neoclassicism into wood in that favorite retreat place of Russian elders: the outlying hermitage or *skit*.

I took a long walk around that skit before going to the Sunday morning liturgy together with my companions on this pilgrimage, Ekaterina Genieva, her husband, and Father Boris Danilenko, the founding librarian of the new theological library in the Danilov Monastery in Moscow. Father Boris had shown us on the way out from Moscow the proposed larger location for his library, the first modern religious library to be set up in Russia since the Bolshevik Revolution, in the buildings of the former Andreevsky Monastery near a new skyscraper building of the Academy of Sciences. After this dedicated man of learning left to take part in the service, I learned that Genieva and her husband had been evangelized and married by a remarkable priest who seemed in many ways to be a prophet of the Russia we had seen emerging: Father Aleksandr Men.

Men was the greatest preacher of his generation. For that very reason he had been sent by the fearful hierarchy of the Brezhnev era to a parish outside of Moscow, where he could not easily affect the intellectuals who flocked to him. There in September 1990 he was murdered with an axe just as he was about to begin ministering to a large academic audience in Moscow. Men was of Jewish origin, and in his last interview before his martyrdom he spoke out eloquently against the neo-authoritarian and anti-Semitic tendencies he saw growing within some church circles. He lamented:

When we believers marked the one thousandth anniversary of the Baptism of Rus, not one word was said about repentance, not one word about the tragedy of the Russian Church, but only rapture and ecstasy about oneself.[67]

Behind the fear of others that underlay negative nationalism in general and anti-Semitism in particular, Men saw a "fear of broad spaces" and a desire for confinement, the very opposite of the storied "broad Russian nature" that he himself represented. His murder—almost certainly at the hands of the same protofascist elements he warned against—was the first harbinger of the reactionary turn that Gorbachev took later in the fall of 1990, bringing into power many of the key figures that made the putsch. Now, with the putsch defeated and our quiet thanks rendered, one of

Men's most fervent followers, Genieva, turned to me and said "forgive me" before she went up to receive the communion wine. As we left the church to make our way back to Moscow, she took an unusually large portion of the communion bread, broke it, and gave me a piece to eat "in memory of Father Aleksandr."

The trip back from Optina represented a return to the reality of the Russian present after a week of exhilarating but unreal immersion in a democratic future and a monastic past. Here again was the mute witness of provincial Russia: decaying collective farms with rusting equipment, baskets of blighted fruit being sold along the road to motorists from the already hungry cities, women in bandanas not as old as they looked taking plastic flowers to the graveyard.

I felt the same sense of renewal that I had experienced a week before the coup on my visit to Tolstoy's estate at Yasnaya Polyana, the simple, social joys of good food and good people in the city of Tula. Returning once again from the region south of Moscow just a week after the coup, I was glad when we stopped off in another provincial city, Kaluga. There was no meal this time, but I had the same satisfaction of sharing food with good people as we ate plums and apples bought along the way and boiled water for tea on a contraption that Genieva's ingenious husband had rigged up through the car's cigarette lighter.

The setting sun lent a special kind of burnished beauty to the largely rusted cupolas of the many churches that dotted the riverside skyline of this frayed but lovely city. But we were specially drawn to the soaring brick Church of St. George, an original creation of the early eighteenth century reached only by high stairs. The small but diverse number of people who were still in the church after all services had ended knew much more about the events in Moscow than the monks in Optina. One old woman said that she had come to her church to thank God for what she had seen on television: "Young people in Moscow are paying honor again to icons of our St. George."

As I took a final walk around this small, soaring church, my eyes were lifted upward to a fresco staring down from the main cupola. The high drum or neck beneath the cupola was filled with windows through which the setting sun poured reddish rays on the face of the Creator in the dome: the classic Pantokrator looking down at his creation from the symbolic vault of heaven in an Eastern Christian church. The face was not severe, as it had previously been in Byzantium; nor was it naturalistic, as it had begun to be in the Westernizing period when the church was built. It was more like the haunting, otherwordly Christ on the icon screens of Rublev and Dionysius, from a time when Russian Orthodoxy was breaking with Byzantium without yet turning to the West. It was a face that had moved beyond suffering into another world, where distance was still bridged with compassion.

It was dark when I finally left that church, and it was still dark when my plane took off for home the following morning. I knew that Russia was heading into colder weather and greater darkness. But it was hard to forget the face I had seen in that last bit of sunshine, and the thought persisted that perhaps this image of compassionate hope had recovered its place in Russian life.

PART FIVE

Retrospect and Prospect

Four visits back to Moscow after the failed coup gave me an opportunity to learn what Russians themselves thought it all meant.

Returning on library business, I found that the Russian cultural institutions with which we had been extensively involved now faced unprecedented new problems.

With the rapid dissolution of the USSR, the subsidy of the central government for all national cultural institutions was simply evaporating. There was great fear that large elements of museum and library collections were being quietly sold off, particularly by corrupt former Communist officials taking cover under the campaign for "privatization." *Privatizatsiia* in this field was often thought to be indistinguishable from *prikhvativatsiia* (ripping off).

At the same time, the victory of democracy in August had increased the popular demands for greater access to the leading libraries and archives, which previously had been largely the privileged preserve of Party-approved figures. The popular clamor was also increasing for access to the "special deposits" (*spetskhrany*) in libraries and to the archives of organizations like the Central Committee of the Party and the KGB that were thought to contain many of the untold secrets of the totalitarian era.

The complex, daunting process of opening these archives took me back repeatedly to Moscow. As the Soviet state followed the Communist Party into oblivion in the final months of 1991, virtually the entire vast written legacy of both institutions was transferred to the Russian Archival

Committee under Rudolf Pikhoya, who was invested with cabinet-level authority. He asked me in October to assemble and coordinate international advice on methods and priorities.

As I met repeatedly with Pikhoya and his associates in the former Central Committee headquarters on Old Square, I was overwhelmed with the task he faced. Walking through miles of subterranean corridors, I saw some of the 75 million items in that archive alone, which had been the operating files of the Central Committee up until the putsch. He was in a difficult position, for his responsibilities were multiplying just as his state subsidy was drying up. Irate Russians were demanding access to all the terrible secrets, while former officials (many still in place) were trying to keep as much secret as possible.

His domain added to the already existing state archives the Central Archives of the Communist Party (with eight volumes of unpublished Lenin items), a Special Archive of wartime trophies (including Goebbels's diary and an archive of the Rothschild family), more than eighty major archives scattered across the country (provincial Party archives, microfilm and audiovisual archives, etc.), some fifty archives from the now-defunct ministries of the former Soviet government (excepting Defense and Foreign Affairs), a Presidential Archive of Politburo-level material that Boldin had assembled in the Kremlin, and the massive archives of the KGB, which were being specially processed by a fifty-person committee of the Russian Parliament under Dmitry Volkogonov as chairman and Pikhoya as vice chairman.

Late in 1991 I convened three meetings in America and England of Western scholars and bibliographers. In December I took to Pikhoya some recommendations that closely resembled those of his own Russian academic advisers. They then suggested a first unveiling of the secrets of the archives in an exhibit at the Library of Congress; and I subsequently worked with them to realize this goal. The exhibit of 300 items opened on June 17, 1992, during the Yeltsin-Bush summit.

Working even as an external adviser with such sensitive matters, I became more aware than ever both of the bold determination of the Russian reformers to enter a new era and of the continued conservative resistance to opening up Russia to the outside world. I was present in the Kremlin late in October, when Yeltsin first presented his bold economic reform to the first full Russian parliament to meet after the coup attempt, the Fifth Congress of People's Deputies. There was almost no applause, and the greatest generation of emotion on that historic occasion was produced in the corridor outside, where the crypto-fascist Vladimir Zhirinovsky was preaching his xenophobic, neo-imperialist message to a large crowd that seemed more fascinated than hostile.[68]

When I discussed the resistance to democratic reform several days later with Yeltsin's closest associate, Gennady Burbulis, and the reformist historian Yury Afanasev, the latter suggested that an upheaval was more likely than the "second putsch" about which there had been repeated rumors ever since August (*bunt odin* rather than *putch dva*).[69] But despite the hardship of a winter of shortages and dramatically rising prices, there was no major social violence within Russia in the months leading up to the first meeting of the Russian parliament in the post-Soviet era, the Sixth Congress of People's Deputies in April 1992. The biggest upheaval seemed to be occurring within the democratic camp itself. Afanasev quarreled with Pikhoya about the archives;[70] partisans of a stronger legislature attacked the concentration of power in the executive branch;[71] older Moscow and St. Petersburg liberals attacked the Sverdlovians and youthful "advisers in pink pants" around Yeltsin; and revelations about the prior extent of KGB influence in all walks of life heightened mutual suspicions.[72]

In such an atmosphere the continued freedom to criticize encouraged many Russians to take a critical second look at the nature of the August putsch itself.

▱ 11 ▱

A Time of Troubles

In the wake of the August events, old structures disintegrated more rapidly than new structures coalesced.[73] Disinherited Communists became more and more outspoken with their view that there had not been a putsch at all, only a peaceful attempt to restore order and sustain some form of union among the republics.

With more time to complain and the democratic right to do so, hard-liners developed the position set forth by Pavlov and Kriuchkov in the preliminary investigation made just after the coup. They also insisted that, because their position had been leaked to the press, the rights of the defendants had been violated and a fair trial made impossible.[74]

The failure of the junta to use force and its general ineptitude increasingly caused many previously apolitical Russians to accept the view that there had been no real conspiracy, but merely a series of clumsy improvisations. Worsening conditions inclined many begrudgingly to acknowledge that the country was still in an "extraordinary situation" that might yet require stronger and more decisive

145

central leadership than the fledgling democratic movement could provide.

Most striking among the second thoughts that surfaced late in 1991 were, however, the florid and often fantastic suggestions that the entire affair was the result of a provocation and conspiracy by the victorious democratic forces themselves. At its crudest level were the seemingly inevitable theories of a Jewish and/or Masonic conspiracy. One cartoon on some subway walls in Moscow again showed a caricatured Jewish figure pulling marionette strings on both Yeltsin and Gorbachev and was labeled *Peres-troika*. (Shimon Peres remains a favorite figure of anti-Semitic propaganda whether or not he is in power.)

Conspiracy theories tended to focus their venom more on the fading figure of Gorbachev than on Yeltsin, reflecting more the old guard's sense of betrayal than any alternative new political strategy. The most comprehensive theory was put forward late in November 1991 by an investigative team from two reactionary journals, *Molniia* (Lightning) and *Chto Delat?* (What is to be done?).[75] It argued that Gorbachev had, in effect, lost almost all his power, was about to be ousted as both General Secretary of the Communist Party and President of the Union, consented to have Yanaev take extraordinary steps to restore order in his absence, and was not as incommunicado as he claimed in the Crimea. Kriuchkov turned Gorbachev's understanding with Yanaev into a broader governmental committee but kept the KGB from taking any action at all. He initially kept the army in the dark but involved the gullible army commander Yazov in a predictably inept military action designed to discredit the army and presumably facilitate a reconsolidation of power by Gorbachev, the KGB, and the Ministry of Internal Affairs under Pugo.

In this view, every clumsy act and imprecise turn of

phrase by the putschists is given some deliberate ulterior meaning. It is implied that Pugo's meeting with Gorbachev in the Crimea on August 16 provided a link between the separate, but equally despicable, motivations of Kriuchkov and Gorbachev. As in many conspiracy theories, key actions are attributed to the dead; the suicide of Pugo is itself seen as an indication that he had the most to hide. The triumphant conclusion of this often ingenious exposé is that there was no conscious attempt to seize governmental power by any of the junta, just a venal desire of the KGB and of Gorbachev's acolytes to enhance their own petty positions.

The real putsch was engineered by the forces in the White House, whose "Plan X" for defense represented the only genuine conspiracy. General Kobets's statement that he had such a plan ready in his safe on the morning of August 19 is seen as proof that the democratic forces themselves planned a putsch and were aided by major treachery in the armed forces.[76] The end result was that Gorbachev stayed in power a little longer by rejoining the forces determined "to sell, betray, and sell out" (*prodavat, predavat, i prodavatsia*) Russia and making inevitable a future popular uprising.

Many came to see the army as the innocent victim of political intrigue, as ordinary soldiers involved in the events belatedly began to tell their story. An entire issue of another right-wing journal was devoted to interviews with the nineteen-year-old driver of the tank involved in the death of the three young men, with his captain, and with the commander of the Moscow Military District. The picture they present is one of peaceful patrols that never intended to attack anyone and became involved in the tragic incident only because the Moscow police failed to accompany them on their mission. They lament that no one has paid public tribute to one of their own comrades who also died in the incident, and they demand a full accounting for the breakdown of civil order, for spreading the rumors that there would be a storming of the White House, and for the access its defenders gained to military ordnance.[77]

In human terms there was a certain credibility and even some appeal to the story of the bewildered young driver, the youngest of seven children, entering Moscow for the first time, trapped in a tunnel on the ring street, more frightened of the crowds than they were of him, trying to fire over their heads, and, finally, falling asleep in another tank as soon as he could get away from his own. In general, the plight of the military returning from Eastern Europe soon after their return from Afghanistan only to find no places to live and decreasing wages and public esteem was clearly providing explosive material for future political unrest. It seemed increasingly likely that elements in the armed forces would eventually assume a hitherto unprecedented direct role in Russian politics. Younger military officers with reactionary views but no involvement in the putsch seemed to be contending for such a role: General Boris Gromov, the charismatic last military commander in Afghanistan; General Albert Makashov, the commander of the Volga–Ural Military District, who had run against Yeltsin for the Presidency of Russia; and the articulate right-wing nationalist Colonel Viktor Alksnis.

Alksnis called for a "third political force" beyond both Communists and democrats, which he designated as "the governmentalists" (GOSUDARSTVENNIKI) using all capital letters to emphasize the urgency of its task of national salvation, in an interview for the new publication of a new party, "The Russian All-peoples Union" (*Rossiisky obshchenarodny soiuz*, or ROS), pledged to "nationalism, governmentalism, and patriotism."[78]

ROS was led by a young and articulate member of the Russian Parliament, Sergei Baburin, whom many considered the most likely leader of any future reactionary nationalist government. The day after the founding of his new crypto-fascist union in Moscow on December 21, its leaders joined Zhirinovsky in a noisy march on the television station in Moscow demanding immediate access to the *efir*. This "march of the hungry lines" occurred on the day I was leaving Moscow once again at the end of my third visit there after the coup. This was—literally—the darkest night of the year, and I thought about the description that an eyewitness had given me the night before of representatives of some 130 cities at the founding conference of ROS wildly applauding Igor Shafarevich's call for a "patriotism of power."[79]

Shafarevich was an academician whose "governmentalist" perspective was, alas, shared by many others in the academy. One of Russia's greatest art historians had told me in all seriousness a year before that all of Russia's troubles had begun when Gorbachev was initiated into a Masonic Lodge by Margaret Thatcher during his first trip to London. I began to wonder in the predawn darkness on my way to Sheremetevo Airport if this increasingly outrageous, yet intellectually fashionable, right-wing opposition to the Yeltsin government foreshadowed the coming victory of an imperial identity over a democratic one in the new Russia.

I took a measure of encouragement from the simple fact that the reactionaries' outcry seemed as unfocused as it was unoriginal: a protest without a program. It had all the mythic qualities of the televised epic of August without either a leader (Yeltsin) or a locus (the White House) for a new legitimacy. The resurgent Russian right wing seemed doomed, like the Old Believers, to protest against the perceived Antichrists in authority. They seemed uninterested even in discussing the real questions any governing party would have to face, let alone in affirming (even nominally, as the junta had done) the need both to sustain a reform program and to provide an alternative authority to preside over them.

Then, suddenly, in the snowy darkness along the road to the airport (still named Leningrad Prospect), our car was stopped by the militia and we were told that we could go no farther because of a curfew on nighttime travel, for which no authority or explanation was given. Obeying this order would ensure my missing my plane; as we waited by the side of the road, I was reminded again how helpless an individual is before arbitrary authority and how relatively easy it still might be to restore such authority in a country with so very few main roads and communication pathways. I would not have been able even to get a car for this predawn drive had it not been for the emergency help of two friendly bibliographers and veterans of the August barricades, Anatoly Petrik and Gennady Popov of the all-union Book Chamber.

As I sat there in Gennady's idling car in the middle of nowhere, I went through the kind of thought process about mundane problems that is the daily fare of Russians: Should we risk running low on gas to keep warm in the car or risk running low on body heat to keep gas in the car? In such cases, a Russian will generally conserve the commodity for the future at the expense of his comfort in the present. But, fortunately for less hardy foreigners like myself, the affable Gennady was able to persuade the officer to let us proceed in his car. I was soon, once more, left alone with my thoughts on another long flight back to America just before Christmas.

The historical analogy that I brooded over this time was not that of a great, all-European turning point like the revolutions of 1848—though the advent of independence for all fifteen of the Soviet Republics had brought self-determination to more previously subjugated nationalities in the fall of 1991 than had the famous "springtime of nations" in 1848. But summer hopes had given way to a winter of discontent. A historian of Russia could not avoid thinking about the more purely Russian and inherently gloomy analogy that Russians themselves used in thinking about the crisis they were going through.

This was for most Russians another *smutnoe vremia*: a Time of Troubles. In its original "Address to the Soviet People" the junta had appealed "to all true patriots, people of good will to put an end to our present time of troubles."[80] After the coup had failed, I asked the greatest living scholar of Old Russia, Dmitry Likhachev, what was the most important single, simple thing currently needed in Russian culture. He suggested a reproduction of the history of Russia by Sergei Platonov, whose specialty was this original *smutnoe vremia*: the period of tumultuous interregnum between Boris Godunov and the first Romanov Tsar. Platonov, the semiofficial historian of the Romanov dynasty, had lived through another time of troubles, the interregnum between tsars and commissars, and died in Stalin's gulag in 1933. His classical analysis of Russia's original Time of Troubles from 1605 to 1613[81] seemed relevant to Russia's situation in early 1992.

The disintegration at the beginning of the seventeenth century of the absolutist empire put together by Ivan III and Ivan IV (the Terrible) resembled the disintegration at the end of the twentieth of the totalitarian empire put together by Lenin and Stalin and centered on the same Moscow Kremlin that the Ivans had built. In both cases stagnation induced by terror combined with the breakdown of a traditional line of authoritarian succession to open the way for a new type of leader to initiate Westward-looking reforms (Boris Godunov/Gorbachev) legitimized by proto-parliamentary bodies (zemsky sobors/revitalized Supreme Soviets).

In Platonov's view, the first or "dynastic" stage of the original Time of Troubles occurred within the imperial leadership of Muscovy, preparing the way inadvertently for a second, "social" stage of the crisis in which central authority broke down amid growing violence from below. To many in Moscow, such a process seemed to be happening as inexorably after the fall of Gorbachev late in 1991 as it had after the death of Boris Godunov early in 1605. Partisans of an authoritarian, xenophobic identity for Russia could take heart from the fact that the social breakdown of stage two was eventually overcome by a broader uprising that ushered in a third, "national" stage. In this stage of reconsolidation, imperial and social unity was reestablished around a new Tsar (Michael, the first Romanov), who installed a new and more stable dynasty that restored most of the old governmental system. More moderate conservatives could use the analogy to argue that the new Tsar was a more limited and constitutional monarch than his predecessors, chosen by a nationwide "council of all the land" (*zemsky sobor*) and watched over by a church in many ways more powerful than the state (with the new title of Patriarch conferred on Tsar Michael's father, Filaret).

But it seemed to me that the analogy of a new Time of Troubles was losing validity just as it was gaining popularity. The original Time of Troubles had been resolved by a national mobilization against a foreign invasion. Polish invaders had occupied the Moscow Kremlin and had moved on to besiege Russia's most sacred national shrine: the Monastery of St. Sergius and the Holy Trinity. This time Russia's neighbors were seeking more to help than to harass, more to steady than to destabilize the Russian state.

Russians had already elected in June and defended in August their own popular alternative to authoritarian rule. Boris Yeltsin—whatever his political life span might prove to be—bore little resemblance to any of the three characters that had struggled to dominate Russia during the troubled interregnum between Boris Godunov and Michael Romanov: the weak and intriguing boyar of the old school Vasily Shuisky, the foreign-sponsored pretender Grigory Otrepev (the false Dmitry), and the leader of the motley rebel upheaval from the countryside, Ivan Bolotnikov.

In Russia of early 1992 there seemed to be neither a credible alternative leader nor a legitimate pretext for an authoritarian nationalist uprising. Lenin had provided the one, and the degradation of World War I the other, for an authoritarian resolution of Russia's last Time of Troubles, the revolutions of 1917 and the subsequent civil war. But the fact that the current crisis was different did not provide any reassurance that the outcome would be positive.

With the resignation of Gorbachev and the formal dissolution of the USSR at the end of 1991, both the alleged victim of the putsch and the government that was preparing to prosecute the putschists simply vanished. In its final reports, the all-union parliamentary commission investigating the August coup observed wryly that it was difficult legally to distinguish between the unsuccessful move against Gorbachev in August and his successful removal in December.[82] As the state prosecutor of the Russian Republic, Valentin Stepankov, took over the criminal investigation from the defunct Soviet government, Russian deputies asked him if all charges would be dropped, since the Soviet Union no longer existed.[83] He was constrained by a vote in the Russian parliament from arresting even someone the commission had implicated in working out specific plans to seize the White House, the former Deputy Minister of Defense Vladislav Achalov.[84] A slackening of interest in punishing the putschists seemed implicit in the commission's finding that only seven of the thirty-two high-ranking KGB officers implicated in the coup had been dismissed (one had even been promoted), while a number of the new republic leaders were shown to have been at least for a time willing to work with the junta (Leonid Kravchuk in Ukraine, Nursultan Nazarbaev in Kazakhstan, and, most strongly, Ayaz Mutalibov in Azerbaijan and Zviad Gamsakhurdia in Georgia).[85]

Whatever the legal judgment might be on those involved in the coup, a political judgment was already possible by the beginning of 1992. The coup was the last in a series of three improvised and increasingly desperate attempts by the Communist political and security machine during 1991 to repress the forces seeking democracy within and independence beyond the Russian Republic. Unlike the attempt to have Yeltsin removed as Russian President in March, 1991,[86] and the attempt to have All-Union Prime Minister Pavlov take over most of Gorbachev's authority as All-Union President in June, the August coup attempt by the Committee on the Extraordinary Situation was not merely rebuffed. It was answered by a counter-coup from the resurgent democratic forces around Yeltsin.

The new Yeltsin government rapidly brought to an end the legal existence of the previously ruling Communist Party and the political-economic dominance of the military–industrial complex. These actions were justified on the basis of evidence that rapidly came to light of structural involvement in the coup by both of those overlapping forces. Although many documents of the central figures in Moscow were destroyed, the takeover of the Central Committee files revealed secret telegrams of August 19 from local Party secretaries that expressed support for the putsch and urged even stronger measures:

We express our serious concern at the absence of a system of permanent control for carrying out in localities the orders of the Extraordinary Committee. We propose that the Committee create a control organ with representatives of the republics, regions, and districts. From our side, we are ready to take part in its work.[87]

Yanaev appears to have been too drunk to destroy a memorandum from the KGB entitled "Regarding certain axioms of the extraordinary situation," dated August 19 and later found in his office. It outlined with a certain cynical brilliance how the junta could consolidate its power. It can be seen in many ways as the last political manifesto of the dying Communist nomenklatura and as such is worth reproducing in full:

1. We must not lose the initiative and enter into any kind of negotiations with the public. They [meaning we] have often ended up doing this in an attempt to preserve a democratic façade. As a result, society gradually becomes accustomed to the idea that they can argue with the authorities—and this is the first step toward the next battle.
2. One must not allow even the first manifestations of nonloyalty: meetings, hunger strikes, petitions, and information about them. On the contrary, they become, as it were, permitted forms of opposition, after which even more active forms will follow. If you want to get along with a minimal amount of bloodshed, suppress contradictions at the very beginning.
3. Do not be ashamed of resorting to clearly expressed populism. This is the law of winning support from the masses. Immediately introduce economic measures that are understandable to all—lowering of prices, easing up on alcohol laws, etc.—and the appearance of even a limited assortment of products in popular demand. In this situation do not think of economic integrity, the inflation rate, or other consequences.
4. One must not delay informing the populace about all

the details of the crimes of one's political opponent. At
first they will avidly search for information. Exactly at
this point one must bring down an information storm of
exposure, the revelation of guilty groups and syndicates,
corruption, and so forth. On other days the information
about one's opponent should be given in an ironically
humorous key: that is, the same [as we used to get from]
those who ruled us. The information must be as graphic
and as simple as possible.
5. One must not crack the whip with direct threats; better
   to start rumors about the strictness of the regime and the
   control of discipline in production and life, as if there
   were systematic raids on stores, places of relaxation, and
   others.
6. One must not be slow in dealing with personnel decisions and reassignments. The population should know
   who is being punished and for what evident reasons; who
   is answering to whom for what; and to whom the population should turn with its problems.[88]

The Yeltsin government followed an almost exactly opposite path after the failed coup, forsaking initial demagoguery in economic policy and vindictive purges of personnel.
By the end of 1991 Yeltsin seemed to have repudiated an
imperial identity for a democratic one, as he joined with the
heads of the other republics in crafting a loose new Com-
monwealth of Independent States in place of a disintegrating Union of Soviet Socialist Republics.

But, as Yeltsin began implementing his program of economic austerity, Russian democracy seemed to be entering
as cold a world as that which the babies placed in outdoor
crèches must have felt during Russia's first public Christmas
pageants since 1916. Yeltsin's decision to bite the bullet of
radical economic reform that Gorbachev had merely nib-

bled at for six years required him to postpone the implementation of a new and genuinely democratic and decentralizing constitution that had been prepared by a commission under Oleg Rumiantsev.[89] The partisans of radical reform who sought to increase Yeltsin's executive powers during the Sixth Congress of People's Deputies in April 1992 were frustrated by the partisans of increased legislative control. But some measure of increased central authority seemed increasingly desirable to many Russians concerned with preventing violence and sustaining basic social services. Once reconsolidation began and new legitimacy developed for strong central authority, would not this create a dynamic leading to dictatorship?

Even before the coup attempt, some had suggested that the three right-wing candidates who polled 35 percent of the votes for President of Russia (against Yeltsin's 57 percent) might prove to be stalking horses for an ostensibly more reasonable military dictator who would "become our Soviet Pinochet."[90] Many looked to Yeltsin's increasingly autocratic Vice President Rutskoi to fulfill this function. Others either feared or hoped that Yeltsin himself might assume such a role.[91] The reduction in size and prestige of the army and claims to parts of it by the newly independent republics led to fears that, as the ultranationalist Aleksandr Prokhanov had prophesied already in 1990, "the army is not a blind function of power. Today it is finding political will."[92]

But the real discovery of political will during these last two turbulent years has been among the younger generation of ordinary Russians, the generation that has grown up since Khrushchev without ever sharing Gorbachev's illusion of that era that Communism could be reformed. The events of August inspired this new generation in particular to believe that Russia could be reformed only by getting rid of Communism.[93] Young soldiers no less than students, priests no less than entrepreneurs felt the exhilaration of living by hope rather than fear, whether or not they had been on the barricades.

They felt pride as Russians that they were now not just more open and free than the Communist nomenklatura, but better people for having defied them. Of all the words spoken from the White House balcony during the crisis, none has lingered in mind more clearly than Elena Bonner's simple words of affirmation to the crowd and defiance to the junta: "We are higher, we are cleaner" (*My vyshe, my chishche*). Even in the cold and hungry winter that followed, there was a feeling that Russians had rediscovered a common consciousness along with their individual consciences.

But how democratic was this awakened national consciousness, and what were the long-run prospects for democracy in Russia? Despite the historic lack of a democratic tradition in Russia, there had been a rapid development of democratic groups and activities in the four short years leading up to August 1991.

The Russian democratic movement began at a deep moral level with the formation in the summer of 1987 of the "Memorial" movement to reexamine and rectify the Communist heritage of repression. Its "week of conscience," with its public "walls of memory" throughout Russia in November 1988, "helped generate and consolidate a new form of civic awareness,"[94] which then fed into the more directly political "popular front" movements. These sprang up at the republic level throughout the USSR as a form of opposition to Communist apparatchik rule that did not go so far as to create a rival "party." These fronts helped organize popular participation in election campaigns involving ever larger numbers of ordinary people and increasing television coverage in the spring of 1989 and the spring of 1990.

Popular fronts in the minority republics soon turned their

attention more to seeking national independence than to reforming the Soviet Union. Those popular fronts thus tended to be implicitly anti-Russian even as they adopted explicitly democratic programs. As if in reaction, the Russian Popular Front that eventually emerged under Valery Skurlatov became implicitly antidemocratic as it defined a distinctively Russian nationalism. Representatives of some fifty Russian regions had met twice during the summer and autumn of 1989 to try to form such a front in the city of Yaroslavl, the site of the famous popular uprising (*opolchenie*) in 1613 that ended the original Time of Troubles and led to a national revival under a new dynasty. But the democratic elements were left out of the much smaller front that Skurlatov created.

The democratic forces came together to create four important new political parties in 1990 after the Communist Party gave up its exclusive "leading role" in February. Superficially they seemed to be replicating both the standard European two-party system (with Christian Democratic and Social Democratic parties) and the American version (with Democratic and Republican Parties).[95] But the real news was their common action, together with a bewildering variety of grassroots organizations from the emerging civil society in the two great election campaigns of 1991 in the Russian Republic: the March campaign that garnered a 70 percent mandate for conducting an unprecedented popular election of a Russian President, and the June campaign that elected Yeltsin.

This mass activity occurred under the leadership of a loose coalition called Democratic Russia, which amounted to a kind of democratic popular front. Elections had created the alternate source of legitimacy to both the Communist Party and the Soviet government that proved so essential in resisting the coup in August. But it was the giant demonstration of March 28 in Moscow against the attempted overthrow of Yeltsin that anticipated and inspired the resistance from below and turned the disparate democratic forces into something that became—quite literally—a movement.

Denied by military force the chance to meet near the traditional sites of power in the center of Moscow, the democratic forces marched instead in a festive way to another location, gathering numbers and solidarity as they moved. The epic of endless Communist success was being challenged by a carnival in the streets, a festivity from below that in August drew a circle around a White House through which the high priests of the old rituals did not dare to pass. But the nagging question grew during this Time of Trouble about whether the carnival spirit of August was the prelude to democracy rooted in law or only to chaos leading to dictatorship.

I had first heard the word "carnival" used to describe Russian reality in August 1990, in a boat on Lake Baikal in the company of the conservative writer Valentin Rasputin. He described the parliament of the USSR in which he was then sitting as a "madhouse," and his friends added the words "circus" and "carnival" in a far less respectful sense than the word had been used by Bakhtin. In the aftermath of the putsch, Rasputin seemed to have concluded that all of Russia had succumbed to such indiscipline and that the only hope for Russia was "the preservation of its governing power [*gosudarstvennost*], the revival of its former glory and honor."[96] Certainly, many Russians who had resisted the Committee on the Extraordinary Situation in 1991 seemed to be looking for something like such a committee to take over in 1992.

Yet whatever was to happen in the short run at the top, something seemed to have changed for the long run at the bottom. The violence from below that everyone had predicted for the long winter did not take place. The age when life could be controlled from on high was over. The carnival had stripped away the epic pretensions of the Soviet era, which had moved from its "iliad" of wartime struggles to an "odyssey" of postwar expansion—even into space.[97] The totalitarian monologue was beginning to give way, as Bakhtin had hoped, to the beginnings of dialogue between discordant views, with the other newly independent states of the former Soviet Union and within Russia itself.

⌧ 12 ⌧

The Dawn of Dialogue

Prior to the coup attempt, I had seen Russia moving simultaneously outward to create new political and economic institutions and inward to recover old cultural and religious values. In the months after the putsch there were many discouraging signs that these paths might never open. Aid from the Western democracies was initially modest, and the newly founded democratic institutions seemed fragile and quarrelsome. Great cultural institutions were impoverished and demoralized (the Russian National Library, formerly the Lenin Library, shut down altogether for a time late in 1991), and the Orthodox Church was weakened by revelations about some of its leaders' past connections with the KGB.[98]

But both the installation of democracy and the recovery of religion may have been taking stronger root than was evident on the surface. This thought occurred to me as I talked in my office in January with Konstantin Lubenchenko, the reform leader who had briefly served as the last speaker of the all-union parliament. He had substituted a Bible for the works of Lenin in his office in the Kremlin and had often quietly visited the Cathedral of the Assumption, whose golden domes gleamed just outside his windows.[99] He had come to America both to attend meetings organized by evangelical Christians and to set up a training center for parliamentary democracy for all the republics of the former Soviet Union. He criticized the precipitous dissolution of the USSR on legal grounds, just as he had opposed the illegality of the August coup. But he was not looking back, and he came armed with endorsements from the legislative and judicial branches of the new Russian government.

Both of those branches of government had shown some signs of independence from the executive branch late in 1991. When in the early autumn Yeltsin impulsively sent troops to quell the independence-minded Chechen Autonomous Republic, the Russian Supreme Soviet overruled him, and he retreated. When, in the early winter, Yeltsin tried to unite the two principal security forces of the Russian government (the reduced KGB with the Russian Ministry of Internal Affairs, MVD), the Russian Chief Justice ruled it unconstitutional and Yeltsin again pulled back.

One of the leading journalistic chroniclers of the August events recalled in November the famous legend that the Russian Decembrists of 1825 thought that *Konstitutsiia* (the unfamiliar Russian word for constitution) was the wife of the Grand Duke Constantine. *Demokratiia* (Democracy), he suggested, is now thought of by Russians as the chattering sister or sister-in-law of Yeltsin. But the relationship of Russians to "her" may be deepening: "Yesterday we welcomed democracy, shrieking out 'Hurrah' at her. Today democracy is demanding from us conjugal fidelity." Thinking people have a special obligation "not to encourage people once again to prefer an effective 'power' to a 'useless' government." Russians must work together for "a normal government of laws."[100]

The courageous journalists of Echo Moscow retrospectively shrugged off the accolades they received for heroism during the August events by speaking of "the heroization of what is normal."[101] General Dmitry Volkogonov, the historian whom Yeltsin appointed to preside over both the declassification of the KGB archives and the organization of a new Russian army, wrote on the eve of the Sixth Congress of People's Deputies in April 1992 that Russia might at last be ready simply "to conduct civilized reforms" in the realization that "it is more useful to measure one's own life not by the dates of leaders' reigns, but by the days and years of one's own accomplishments."[102] Although the proceedings of that congress were tempestuous, the net result was an agreement to continue with economic reform, rejecting any sharp move either to increase or to curtail Yeltsin's presidential powers. A new constitution was not enacted, but the text was opened up for nationwide popular suggestions. The process to provide the basis for a new government that could conduct Russia's first post-Communist elections and produce a truly representative body free of holdovers from the nomenklatura seemed to be under way at last.

But could Russia in search of a post-Communist identity harmonize its strivings toward liberal, pluralistic democracy with its search to recover conservative, religious authority? Many of the participants in the defense of the White House, such as Viktor Aksiutich in Moscow and Ilya Konstantinov in St. Petersburg, became appalled at the seeming loss of central authority in Russia under democratic leadership. They sought to lead a new "center-right" opposition to the Yeltsin government, apparently believing that they could control their new ultranationalist and crypto-fascist allies rather than be controlled by them.

The sense that Russia was being humiliated under democratic leadership was shared even by many who stayed with Yeltsin. The relatively liberal Metropolitan Cyril of Smolensk received a warm ovation from a congress of army officers in the Kremlin Palace of Congresses on January 17 with his suggestion that the political separation of Russia from Ukraine and Belorus shattered "the commonalities of a thousand years." Although he defended the wisdom of "voluntary self-limitations on governmental power," he denounced the "politics of radical sovereignty," which "separates children from parents, creates boundaries between man and wife."[103] Atheistic Marxist professors publicly implored the Patriarch to rally the forces of central authority against the social disintegration that democracy was bringing.[104] Aksiutich, as the lead speaker at a rally of his newly formed Gathering of the Russian People (*Rossiiskoe Narodnoe Sobranie*), demanded the removal of the Yeltsin government on April 5 in Manezh Square on the eve of the Sixth Congress of People's Deputies.

When Yeltsin's reformist forces came early that morning to the auditorium of the Rossiia Hotel for a kind of preparatory pep rally before the Congress, they were forced to run a gauntlet of reactionary protesters flaunting the flags and singing the songs of the defunct Soviet Union along with a motley array of nationalist and anti-Semitic placards. They pelted delegates with coins for having "sold out" Russia before moving over to join Aksiutich's rally in Manezh Square—ostensibly to commemorate the 750th anniversary of Aleksandr Nevsky's famous victory on the ice over the Teutonic knights.

Lacking the necessary credentials for entry into the Yeltsin meeting, I had to run the gauntlet several times and thus had plenty of chances to see how a number of young people had attached themselves in a festive spirit to the relatively small number of hard-core organizers. They were shouting "Yeltsin to Siberia," not realizing perhaps that that was his political base. In a way, the reactionaries were finally having a carnival of their own. The reformers were now the establishment, meeting indoors and rhythmically

165

chanting *nuzh-no, nuzh-no* (we must, we must) when a delegate proposed excluding all former members of the nomenklatura from high government positions for the next few years. The reactionaries were meeting outdoors for their own counter-carnival. It assembled in Gorky Park, then paraded down to the Manezh in imitation of the reformist processions of the previous year.

But there was a hard edge to this carnival. Coins thrown at close range injured the eyes of a woman running the gauntlet just ahead of me. There was genuine hate in the eyes of the organizers of the demonstration, former Communists who had become crypto-fascists, the so-called "red-browns." The lawyer preparing the defense for the former head of the KGB, Kriuchkov, announced at a Moscow reception early in April that there would be a million demonstrators in the streets of Moscow the day his client was put on trial. As the democrats proceeded to fight with each other in the April Congress, the fear that ultranationalism would fill the ideological vacuum left by the death of Communism and would enable former Communist officials to return to power under new banners remained not far below the surface.

The speaker of the Russian Parliament, Ruslan Khasbulatov, sought to clip Yeltsin's wings in less violent ways than the red-brown movement. Khasbulatov was from the small Chechen minority within the Russian Federation, and seemed anxious to establish his credentials as a Russian nationalist with increasingly sharp attacks on Yeltsin. By May 1992, friends reported that these two, who lived close to each other and had maintained good human relations in the Russian bath that they shared together, were no longer speaking to each other even in that hitherto apolitical place. But in his opening address to the Congress on April 6 Khasbulatov had spoken of the need for "dialogue," turning my thoughts to Bakhtin's theory of dialogue—his suggestion that the spirit of the carnival had migrated through the novels of Dostoevsky into modern life.

A lifetime of studying Dostoevsky had convinced Bakhtin that the novel was a wellspring of innovation. It was an "open" genre that broke the hold of autocratic "monologue" in favor of a new kind of dialogue between people with deeply divergent views, in effect, prefiguring the pluralism of authentic convictions needed in modern societies. Bakhtin seemed to suggest that, just as the epic mode had been superseded by the broader possibilities of the novel, so autocracy was giving way to democracy. It seemed appropriate that the two humanistic critics most deeply involved in the defense of the White House during those August days were perhaps Russia's greatest living interpreters of Bakhtin (Viacheslav Ivanov) and of Dostoevsky (Yury Kariakin) and that Afanasev's new Humanistic University was preparing to set up a Bakhtin Institute.

But where were the novelists themselves—those who could continue the cleansing role in society that Bakhtin had attributed to them? Rasputin, one of the best, had given up fiction for polemics. Like most of the other "village writers" who had dominated Russian fiction in recent years, Rasputin was engaging in the politics of nostalgia and cultural despair: the classic breeding grounds for fascist-type ideologies.

One of Rasputin's erstwhile collaborators from Irkutsk, the mathematician Viktor Trostnikov, introduced me in Moscow in December 1991 to the work of a younger writer from the same Siberian city, Leonid Monchinsky. His first novel, *Absolution Sunday* was Dostoevskian in its empathy for variety as well as in its religious themes.[105] Trostnikov saw in this work the suggestion of a way out of Russia's *smuta* through "creative repentance."[106]

This seemed to me a good way to describe what Rudolf Pikhoya was trying to do for his country by opening up the archives of a dark past. It seemed appropriate that Pikhoya had written his dissertation on the doctrine of repentance in medieval Russian canon law.

"Today's time of repentance is a crisis after which renewal and purification will come," the poet-novelist Olesia Nikolaeva had written already in February 1990.[107] The events of August accelerated these transforming human processes. Nikolai Stolyarov, an air force officer promoted to be Vice Chairman of the KGB after the defeat of the putsch, told a visiting delegation of American Christian evangelists in the fall of 1991 that "political questions cannot be decided until there is sincere *repentance*, a return to faith by the people."[108]

August 1991 was the moment of shared social catharsis that for many preceded and made possible the *pokaianiia* (repentance) and *ochishchenie* (cleansing) that people began to experience individually. Prior to the coup, I had seen the future dependent on whether Russia would experience a nationalistic catharsis (promising to cleanse Russia of foreign impurities by purging scapegoats and creating a new authoritarianism) or a moral catharsis of repentance and redemption. The latter is a spiritual process compatible with pluralistic democracy, since it looks within and above for a positive identity rather than without and below for a common enemy. Having experienced in the 1930s a negative catharsis far worse than anyone then thought possible, Russia in the 1990s may have embarked on a more positive catharsis than anyone now can imagine.

Even more than elsewhere in Eastern Europe, where Communist rule was less brutal and long-lived, post-Communist Russia seemed remarkably free of retroactive vindictiveness toward individuals. Most Russians did not even seem unduly eager to bring the junta to trial, let alone punish them. There was a sense that almost everyone had been implicated in the moral degradation of Communism and was now involved in his or her own process of self-cleansing.

After a long seminar and conversation with the elderly Russian priest Vitaly Borovoi (whose long service abroad had inevitably raised suspicions of parallel involvements with Soviet authorities) in Geneva in September 1991, he told me with tears in his eyes that he had experienced "a catharsis." I remembered with new appreciation how he had told a hostile emigré audience in a Paris conference on the Millennium of Russian Christianity in 1988 that the true history of the Russian Church in the Soviet era would have to be based on the lives of hundreds of parish priests whom no one knew anything about. This formed a marked contrast with the only other Russian clerical presentation at that conference: Metropolitan Pitirim's cinematic display of the luxurious restoration of his cathedral in Volokolamsk.

Yet even Pitirim seemed to be suffering from some kind of inner turmoil as I watched him standing ashen and alone at the far right side of the Uspensky Cathedral in the Krem-lin, refusing to take part in a liturgy on April 4 when the Patriarch for the first time canonized some of the church's martyrs from the Soviet era (the long neglected *novo-mucheniki*, or "new martyrs"). Pitirim was silent as well on the next-to-last day of my April visit, when I sat with him in a board meeting of the Cultural Fund as its President, Dmitry Likhachev, spoke eloquently of the need to strengthen provincial cultural activities.

On the last day of my April visit I again went out to the country in the company of Genieva and Levner to visit both the home and the church of the man many expected some-day to be added to the list of "new martyrs": the late Father Aleksandr Men. Both the young priest who succeeded him and his musician son told me they had grown closer to him since his death; and in his reverently preserved, book-lined study I felt the continued presence of a figure who had somehow overcome the old tension in Russian culture between priests and intellectuals. The cupolas of the mother monastery of Muscovy, St. Sergius and the Holy Trinity, were visible from the path on which he was battered with an axe. He had bled to death at the gate of his house; one had to step over his body, at least in imagination, to enter. On the wall of his study was a special icon of Byzantium's great preacher, St. John Chrysostom, known as "the blessed silence."

The Church, like Russian society at large, was being transformed from the bottom up and not from the old structures of power on the top, which young seminarians referred to as the *Mitropolitburo*.[109] The simple new message was one of love and hope in a society long ruled by hate and fear. Father Zinon, the greatest of modern icon painters and the closest modern equivalent to Dostoevsky's idealized Russian monk, warned after the coup that Orthodoxy was at a crossroads.[110] It could either become a state-controlled religion as it had been one way or another from the time of Peter the Great through the Soviet period, or it could recover its vitality and independence by developing a new life of prayer, hard work, and Christian education. The key was a renewed local community (*obshchina*) where private property would be sacred and individual rights not lost in the collective.

Such a vision was similar to that of other Christian denominations in Russia. It was not merely compatible with, but conducive to, democratization. Father Zinon had painted the frescoes for the restored Danilov Monastery in Moscow; Father Boris Danilenko had collected its books and was taking duplicates to those young monks at Optina who had continued to sing their offices oblivious to what was going on the past August. In their own way, these young clerics were providing the broader society with models for the kind of discipline and dedication that would be needed to turn the carnival spirit of the barricades into the hard everyday labor needed to build their new ideal of a "normal society."

In a parliamentary discussion of the putsch on February 18, 1992, a reactionary made fun of the new linkage of democracy with religion, implying that there had been more moral discipline in the old Communist order. General Kobets, the defender-in-chief of the White House, told the speaker not to engage in "any talk here about morality":

I was here at the time of the putsch and did not see here a single Communist general, but I did see democratic priests among the democrats—not only in the hall, but on the rooves, the barricades, everywhere. [111]

The August events were a breakthrough more to hope than to faith. The young took the lead and did not seem likely to forget—the grandson of Semion Budenny, Stalin's special friend and organizer of the original Red Army cavalry; the son of Aleksandr Yakovlev, the former Politburo member;[112] and two daughters of Stepan Volk from the Marx-Engels-Lenin Institute, both of them converts to Catholicism. There were also more than a few hooligans, as the junta had claimed. But all were treated as equals, behaved in an orderly way, and were willing to follow orders.

The lines that symbolized the inefficiency of everyday life and the helplessness of the individual in Soviet society did not go away with the collapse of Communism. But the memory of the magic circle they had formed in August sustained the hope that a new beginning was really possible. In February, many of those who had defended the White House came back together and named themselves "the living ring" (zhivoe koltso).

There was some solid basis for hope, because Russians in August had discovered not only freedom but responsibility.

They were forced to accept the responsibility for moral choices that had always been avoided in the Communist era. When Likhachev was later asked if he knew the putsch would fail when he spoke out against it on August 20, he replied that he knew only "on whose side is the truth":

If I had spoken out because I was certain that the government would prevail over the putchists, it would have had no moral meaning.[113]

Inspired by people like Likhachev, Russians were recovering a moral sense, reinventing a moral vocabulary, and—in increasing numbers—accepting responsibility to a God that Marxism had tried to stamp out.

Many Russians thought of the August days as a "heroic deed" (*podvig*) of the kind traditionally performed by saints no less than warriors, but for many if not most of the participants it was just their ordinary response to a truly extraordinary situation. The state committee that the Leninist machine had created to deal with that situation had simply been overtaken by a "spontaneously beginning transformation . . . issuing forth from the depths within people . . . with the aim of creating democratic space."[114] In place of the Soviet claim that utopia could be created by those who normalized heroism, Russians now listened to the ironic disclaimer of Echo Moscow against "the heroization of normality": accepting excessive praise for simply doing "what should have been done."[115]

But how could such a simple moral impulse prevail against the largest organized armed force in the history of the world? The proceedings of the parliamentary investigation of the attempted putsch makes it clear that a far greater amount of that strength than was realized at the time was in fact mobilized and deployed around Moscow in August 1991. The junta clearly believed that a massive military procession would have the same intimidating effects as Soviet armored parades in Red Square. The writer Vasily Rozanov has described how he was seduced by a similar unending parade of cavalry through Petersburg in 1903:

> . . . my "ego" was blown like a piece of down into the whirlwind of that enormousness and that crowd. . . . All of a sudden I started to feel that I was not only afraid of, but fascinated by them. . . . I did not look at any specific face [but] to a mass, both human and horse [which] invoked in me the purely womanish sentiment of spineless obedience and an insatiable desire to "be around," to look, to gaze [like] a girl falling in love.[116]

The democratic uprising of August 1991 broke Russia away from this attitude, which Nicholas Berdiaev later described as the "eternally womanish" (*vechno babe*) aspect of the Russian character. But much of the strength to resist the military forces of the coup came, as we have seen, precisely from those long-suffering, often invisible "eternal women" of ordinary Russian life: the babushkas who talked with the soldiers.[117] As these women acted like "men," the men in the tanks began to feel something of Rozanov's "womanish" desire simply to "be around" people who were very much like their mothers.

Force has always required some higher legitimacy in Russia. The heroes of Russian folk tales always consulted with older people and independent sources of moral authority before entering battle, "thus sharing with them a responsibility for the results."[118] In the world of legend where many Russians are still at home, moral force prevails over material forces—and the retelling of a heroic tale becomes in itself a moral force for the community of listeners. Russia was at last listening to its women. But the events of August were not the work of any particular category of people or of any individual person bigger than life.

Western social scientists generally see the world in terms

of rivalries between political personalities and economic interest groups; but they will probably look in vain for "rational actors" computing the "correlations of forces" amidst all the confusion. The poet Yevtushenko likened the events of August to a fairy tale; and a Ukrainian cultural historian has reminded us that "Russian fairy tales are closer to the traditional subjects of ancient Greek mythology rather than to Western 'individualistic' stories."[119]

The breakthrough of Yeltsin's Russia resembled in broad outline those that had already occurred in Walesa's Poland and Havel's Czechoslovakia. It was an "internal victory over internal fears" producing a "breakout" that was at one level "a wonder, a miracle"; but, at another, simply "the unforeseeable action of the human heart."[120]

This action continues, and its consequences cannot be predicted any more than they can be prevented. People change at different times in different ways; but even the pioneers of perestroika like Aleksandr Yakovlev, who had hoped that change could be handled by Communists and confined to the social and economic spheres, recognized early in 1992 that Russia was undergoing "the deepest kind of transformation" from "cadre politics" to a "new spiritual reality."[121] The moral high ground had been taken over by a new generation seeking not just to construct a "normal society" like others in "the civilized world," but also to write a new chapter in Russian history worthy of their writers' dreams, their soldiers' sacrifices, and their women's prayers.

Of course, no one could say whether, or for how long, the risen hopes of that young generation could be suppressed by a still fearful elder generation. As the summer of 1992 began, cynicism was great, corruption was increasing, political conflict was in the open; and there was some nostalgia for the relative order and predictability of the Communist era. The near-term prognosis seemed ominous.

Yet Russia had survived its first winter in freedom without either of the two forms of destabilizing violence that many foreign experts had predicted: either some internal social uprising caused by economic hardship within Russia or some external conflict with one of the other newly independent republics caused by national animosity between Russians and non-Russians. Russia's horizons seemed somehow to be widening even as its borders contracted. Russians had been released in August from the fear of power to discover the power of hope.

Havel has written that "hope is definitely not the same thing as optimism. It is not the conviction that something will turn out well, but the certainty that something makes sense, regardless of how it turns out."[122] Opening archives and a tumultuous free press were beginning to make sense out of the Russian enigma. The final figure on solid wood inside the *matroshka* may all along have been simply that of an ordinary Russian in search of a responsible government and a free society. Whatever setbacks might lie on the difficult path ahead, I felt strangely certain that an altogether different Russia would be blooming in both faith and freedom by the beginning of the Third Millennium.

The violent twentieth century ended as it had begun, with guns in August. But unlike the massive imperial artillery barrages that opened the first World War in August 1914, the Cold War ended in August 1991 with all guns silent. They had been swept up into a carnival of hope at the heart of the last of the empires, and covered with flowers on the Feast of the Transfiguration.

Acknowledgments

I owe special thanks for support of the research for this work to Dr. David Hamburg and the Carnegie Corporation of New York. I am also grateful for special assistance to a number of colleagues in the Library of Congress, particularly Dr. Irene Steckler and Harry Leich, and to a research assistant, Sarah Despres. I have a deep and special debt to the head of the Library of Congress's Moscow office, Mikhail Levner, and to the deputy head of the Library of Foreign Literature in Moscow, Ekaterina Genieva.

I am grateful to a great many Russians and a number of Western observers for sharing their impressions, thoughts, and documentation with me during and after these events, and I extend sincere thanks to all of them—above and beyond the formal credit I have tried to give in my notes section.

I also thank Dmitry Mamleev for arranging a valuable trip to Siberia in the summer of 1990, President and Mrs. Ronald Reagan for the privilege of accompanying them to the Moscow summit of 1988, and many members of Congress who have encouraged me to continue following things

Russian even while working for America's library. I especially thank the four heads of congressional delegations who asked me to accompany them on official trips in recent years: Senators Claiborne Pell and Bennett Johnston, Speaker Thomas Foley, and former Representative John Brademas. As always, I owe most of all to my family: my wife Marjorie and our children, especially Tom; and I dedicate this book to our grandchildren.

Notes

In these notes, as in the text, I have slightly modified the usual transliteration of Russian (eliminating soft signs, rendering terminal adjectival endings as y, etc.) and have left proper names in the form already familiar in English. I use the abbreviation LC to indicate that unpublished materials referenced herein may be found in the special archive gathered for this project and to be deposited in the Library of Congress.

1. For the originality of Russian terrorism, the positive use of the term in the 1870s, and its legacy to Leninism, see James H. Billington, *Fire in the Minds of Men: Origins of the Revolutionary Faith* (New York, 1980), pp. 405–9.

2. The deepest and best early account of the putsch is by Yury Sidorenko, a physician and deputy to the Supreme Soviet of the Russian Republic, who arrived in Moscow to participate in the Congress of Compatriots and was one of the first to join Yeltsin for the entire three days inside the White House. *Tri dnia, kotorye oprokinuli bolshevizm: Ispoved svidetelia, pokazaniia ochevidtsa* (Rostov-na-Donu: Periodika Dona, 1991), 88 pp.

   Postfactum, which remained fully operational during the three days and carried communication with both the White House and the rest of the USSR, combined with the Russian Information Agency to publish

179

their dispatches as soon as the putsch was defeated, along with some pictures and interpretive material: *Putch: Khronika trevozhnykh dnei*, with prefaces by Andrei Vinogradov and Gleb Pavlovsky (Moscow: Progress, 1991), 286 pp. Most of this material was also published in English in a looseleaf series published by Postfactum and the Interlegal Center for Analytical Review: *The State of the Union*, no. 9, August 22, 1991. The Russian Information Agency also published an hour-by-hour chronology of the three days: *Khronika putcha: Chas za chasom*, (Leningrad: Lenizdat, 1991), 96 pp.

A good immediate journalistic account was in the special issue of *Newsweek*, September 2, 1991. Robert Cullen, "Report from Moscow," *The New Yorker*, November 4, 1991, pp. 54–89, adds testimony from military leaders just below the top level who resisted the coup. Jeff Trimble and Peter Vasiliev, "Three Days That Shook the World," *U.S. News and World Report*, November 18, 1991, pp. 54–67, add details about the junta and raises doubts about Gorbachev's version of his own role. Stuart Loory and Ann Imse, *Seven Days That Shook the World* (Atlanta, 1991), point out in this CNN publication (on the basis of a KGB phone log) that Gorbachev had a number of conversations with Kriuchkov and others of the junta on the first day of the coup (p. 52) and have excellent Tass pictures of the entire period, as well as a good chronicling of the role of the media (pp. 99–102, and the discussion by Nicholas Daniloff, pp. 233–35). Lawrence Elliott and David Satter, "Three Days That Shook the World," *Reader's Digest*, January 1992, pp. 60–66, 177–203, provide an account particularly rich in details on the three young men killed in the resistance.

Material published in the Soviet press about the coup attempt is gathered in *Avgust-91* (Moscow: Politizdat, 1991). A full political chronology for 1991 is in *Nezavisimaia Gazeta*, January 3, 1992, pp. 4–5. The stenographic reports of the commission of the Russian parliament investigating the putsch under L. A. Ponomarev are in LC and identified here by individual titles and dates. Facsimilies of publications of August 19–21 are in *The Coup: Underground Moscow Newspapers*, Minneapolis, 1991.

By far the best of the overall assessments in the flood of instant commentary at the time was that of George Kennan on the *MacNeil/Lehrer Newshour*, August 22, 1991, transcript, pp. 6–9. Among the more interesting later interpretations are Martin Malia, "The Yeltsin Revolution," *The New Republic*, February 10, 1992, pp. 21–25; Slava Len, "Perevorota ne bylo!" *Stolitsa*, no. 39, 1991, pp. 5–7; and Leonid Radzikhovsky, "Tri dnia, kotorye unichtozhili imperiiu," *Stolitsa*, no. 37, 1991, pp. 8–11.

3. The lecture, "Rossiia v poiskakh sebia," was published in *Nezavisimaia*

Gazeta, June 4, 1991, translated and slightly updated (along with a brief account of the protest over it) in *The Wilson Quarterly,* Autumn 1991, pp. 58–65. I discuss here the inadequacy of the term "revolution" to describe these changes—as does Ernst Kux in a work also written before the coup attempt: "Revolution in Eastern Europe—Revolution in the West?" *Problems of Communism,* May–June 1991, pp. 7–13. Kux draws on the neglected work of his fellow Swiss, Jakob Burckhardt, emphasizing the decisiveness of cultural factors in accelerating and determining the outcome of a long-delayed crisis.

4. "Obrashchenie k Sovetskomu Narodu," dated August 18, published in *Pravda,* August 20, 1991, cited as reprinted in *Avgust-91,* pp. 20, 24.

5. Text of the press conference, held in the Press Center of the Ministry of Foreign Affairs, is published in *Avgust-91,* pp. 43–61.

6. Semion Kordonsky, "Pervy voenny perevorot v SSSR," in *Putch: Khronika,* p. 243, based on a radio account of an interview with Lukianov during the second day of the putsch. On the Crimean confrontation, see the account of Gorbachev's aide Anatoly Cherniaev, "Four Desperate Days," *Time,* October 7, 1991, pp. 28–29.

7. A detailed account of these preparations is contained in the LC copy of the stenographic report of the Russian parliament's investigative commission on the putsch, chaired by L. A. Ponomarev: *Uchastie rukovodiashchiego sostava Vooruzhennykh Sil v gosudarstvennom perevorote 19–21 avgusta 1991 goda,* February 18, 1992, pp. 110 ff. This report shows that the size and elaborateness of the military operation were much greater than previously assumed. See pp. 118 ff.

8. "Potomstvo tiskalos k perilam . . ." Boris Pasternak, "Na rannikh poezdakh" (1941), *Izbrannoe v dvukh tomakh* (Moscow, 1985), vol. 1, p. 363.

9. Kordonsky, "Pervy voenny perevorot," *loc. cit.,* p. 242; from a poll in *Glasnost,* August 1991, no. 32.

10. Boldin propagated the idea of an "Academy of the Book" in a high-minded article for Western consumption ("Libraries are the Cradle of our Liberties," *Elan,* July 5–7, 1991, p. 26), and he subsequently sent me (as I had requested in June) a written description of the proposed Academy. This appears to be the successor to earlier plans for a Presidential Library for Gorbachev, which had been floated earlier in the year to a group of us by former Ambassador Anatoly Dobrynin and to me personally by Vice Foreign Minister Vladimir Petrovsky. I discussed both ideas again with Petrovsky in Moscow a week before the coup. Possibly related to either or both of these ideas was the concurrent accumulation of massive materials from the General Section of the Communist Party Central Committee

Archives (which Boldin had controlled for ten years) into a "Presidential Archive" of sensitive materials in the Kremlin.

The Presidential Library idea appears to have been based on both American precedent and on Mitterand's idea of a new Bibliothèque de France. The proposal for an Academy of the Book was revived after the coup by Mayor Gavriil Popov of Moscow.

11. Text, taken from his reading in English during the *MacNeil/Lehrer News-hour*, August 27, 1991, reprinted in *Christian Science Monitor*, September 5, 1991, p. 19.

12. "Komu davat sviatogo Georgiia? Barrikadnaia Mozaika," *Put*, no. 7/10, 1991, p. 3.

13. Text of an interview with Alpha Group Commander Mikhail Golovatov and Deputy Commander Sergei Goncharov, *Rossiiskaia Gazeta*, August 28, 1991, p. 1; English version in FBIS-SOV-91-171 (September 4, 1991), pp. 32–34.

14. Text of Russian TV interview with Yeltsin in the White House on August 25, in FBIS-SOV-91-165 (August 26, 1991), pp. 70–74, esp. pp. 71–72.

15. Detailed article on Kriuchkov and the Alpha unit by V. Filin in *Komsomolskaia Pravda*, August 28, 1991, p. 4, translated in FBIS-SOV-91-171 (September 4, 1991), pp. 34–37.

16. FBIS-OV-91-171, p. 32. In reality there seem never to have been more than three hundred fully armed people inside the White House, and there were probably even fewer during the first evening. General Kobets estimated that "there were about 150 professional military officers in the building." *Avgust-19*, p. 198.

17. Mikhail Bakhtin, *Rabelais and His World* (Cambridge, Mass., 1968), p. 10. This classic work offended the Communist establishment when it was first produced as a doctoral dissertation in 1946 with its theory of the carnival. The degree was denied, and the book not published in Russian until 1965.

18. Vladimir Zviglianich, "Realnost i smysl: mirovozzrencheskie printsipy perestroiki myshleniia: I. Smysl i 'karnavalnost' perestroiki," *Filosofskaia i Sotsiologicheskaia Mysl*, no. 11, 1991, pp. 75–88; as well as his forthcoming "Carnival and Dialogue: Some Views on Perestroika," "At the Carnival of Perestroika," and the longer manuscript that this Kiev scholar has been preparing at the Woodrow Wilson Center during 1991–92.

19. Mikhail Bakhtin, *Problems of Dostoevsky's Poetics* (Minneapolis, 1984), p. 124. This was his first published work (in 1929). It was radically revised and expanded after much personal suffering in exile in a second edition of 1963.

20. The detailed account of the meetings attempting to coordinate military

operations on the twentieth make it clear that Akhromeev, Gromov, and others not formally implicated in the coup attempt were frequent participants. See *Uchastie*, February 18, 1992, pp. 125 ff. There had also been a project to divert Yeltsin's plane from his August 18 flight back to Moscow from Alma Ata and to take him prisoner then. *Ibid.*, p. 131.

21. The demonstrations of striking bus drivers and of crowds around the television station in Nizhny Novgorod seem to have had a particularly festive quality, judging from the pictures and description in N. Stepnoi, "Gosudarstvenny perevorot: Vzgliad iz provintsii," *Volia Rossii*, no. 5–6, 1991, p. 3.

22. Mr. Geh did issue a statement of support for democratization later when the outcome was clear. But he had been for some time the object of bitterness among some rank-and-file librarians in the Soviet Union, as visiting Western dignitaries often are when they seem to have internalized the kind of anticipatory deference to the Communist power elite that ordinary citizens themselves have overcome. Reformist librarians had staged a strike that lasted five months to get rid of a nomenklatura-designated director of the Library of Foreign Literature, only to see that person placed on the central council of the International Federation of Library Associations. They had then sent messages of explanation and protest to Mr. Geh as chairman of the federation, to which they never received any response. Mr. Geh told me in August 1991 that he had never received any such messages, though a number of the Russian librarians indicated that he had previously given them clear indications in conversations that he had received this information.

23. At first, the armored personnel carriers bringing in the troops from the Tula Division were not admitted to the White House because of fear of a "Trojan Horse." See Sidorenko, *Tri dnia*, p. 16, and also pp. 46–47 for an excellent, succinct account of how the resistance was stuctured within the White House; Yeltsin's own account to the Russian Parliament on August 21, in *New York Times*, August 22, 1991, p. A12; and Bruce Auster, "The Military Chooses Sides," *U.S. News and World Report*, November 19, 1991, p. 66. For a different, though not necessarily contradictory, version in which Lebed spoke to Kobets, see Cullen, "Report," pp. 75–76.

24. Cited in Sidorenko, *Tri dnia*, p. 30. Emphasis added in accordance with my memory of her emphasis at the time.

25. Cited in *ibid.* For a preliminary analysis of the legal questions involved in the coup, see Nina Beliaeva and Anatoly Kovler, "Pravo i politika v dni perevorota," in *Putch*, pp. 248–63. The most loudly applauded speech at the largest demonstration of resistance to the coup in the USSR (Dmitry

Likhachev's address in Senate Square in St. Petersburg on August 20) sounded the same theme, as Likhachev rejected the junta's claim to be "leader-instructors" (*rukovoditeli*) of the Russian people: "Such positions and titles are not in our constitution. Leader-instructors for gangs? That is another story." Cited from Likhachev's unpublished memoir of the putsch period and notes for his remarks, *Sobytiia 18–21 Avgusta 1991 g.*, p. 4, kindly provided by the author, in LC.

26. See the section "Deputat Rumiantsev," in "Komu davat sviatogo Georgiia?" *Put*, no. 7/10, 1991, p. 3.

27. For more details on Lubenchenko's role, see James H. Billington, "The True Heroes of the Soviet Union," *New York Times*, August 30, 1991, p. A23. Rumiantsev and Lubenchenko were among the youngest elected delegates to their respective Supreme Soviets, and both had worked effectively at the Library of Congress. Lubenchenko had headed one of the first important delegations to come to study our infrastructure for support of the U.S. Congress and its lawmaking functions in 1989. After the coup he recounted to me in his office the important role in the resistance to the putsch that almost every member of that delegation had played. Rumiantsev had worked on his constitutional project in the Library of Congress for much of the summer of 1990, drawing (as did several hundred other Russians from the USSR in 1990–91) on both the Library's general collections and its Congressional Research Service and Law Library.

28. Sidorenko, *Tri dnia*, pp. 12–13.

29. Accounts of Rudolf Pikhoya from within the White House and of Leonid Ivanov from outside.

30. Abridged transcript in *New York Times*, August 23, 1991, p. A11.

31. Boris Pasternak, "Na rannikh poezdakh," *Izbrannoe*, vol. 1, p. 363. "Moskva vstrechala nas vo mrake, / perekhodivshchem v serebro . . ."

32. Professor Jerry Hough, in transcript of *MacNeil/Lehrer Newshour*, August 27, 1991, p. 6. He saw Yeltsin as "extremely dangerous" and Gorbachev as "able to create the kind of checks and balances he had before."

33. Lead article by Francis Clines, *New York Times*, August 24, 1991, p. 1.

34. Text in *Washington Post*, August 25, 1991, p. A27.

35. I suggested early in 1987 that Solidarity, then still in eclipse, would prove prophetic of the future because of its spontaneity, its bottom-up organization, its links with religion, and its nonviolent dedication to an evolutionary end. I speculated that in the twenty-first century "even in the Soviet Union, historians will look back on Solidarity as an anticipation if not a prototype of movements that they have independently developed to transform their own societies in ways radically different from the violent, secular revolutionary movements of the past." "Introduction" to Steve

Reiquam, ed., *Solidarity and Poland: Impacts East and West* (Washington, D.C., 1988), pp. 1–4. More recently Lawrence Goodwyn, *Breaking the Barrier: The Rise of Solidarity in Poland* (New York/ Oxford, 1991), p. 390, credits Solidarity with "setting in motion the dynamics that liberated not only Eastern Europe, but the Soviet Union itself."

36. Transcript of *MacNeil/Lehrer Newshour*, August 27, 1991, p. 11.

37. An extended tribute to Rostropovich as "the living incarnation of a higher spirit" in their midst is in Sidorenko, *Tri dnia*, pp. 18–19.

38. Cited in lead story by Michael Dobbs in *Washington Post*, August 27, 1991, p.1.

39. Title of article by David Remnick in *Washington Post*, August 25, 1991, p. 1.

40. Sidorenko, *Tri dnia*, p. 53 on the Russian parliament; p. 67 on the all-union Congress; and pp. 48 ff. on the broader moral issues.

41. A substantial excerpt from this impromptu talk was transcribed and published in *Literaturnaia Gazeta*, September 11, 1991.

42. S. Na'aman, *Lassalle* (Hanover, 1970), pp. 125–78, esp. p. 127. Marx's idea that a journal should create and enforce "party spirit" was the direct ancestor of Lenin's concept of *partiinost* or sacrificial party spirit. See Billington, *Fire in the Minds of Men*, p. 318 and, for the 1840s, "The Magic Medium Journalism," pp.306–23.

43. Sobchak's excellent account of his role in the coup is in his *For a New Russia: The Mayor of St. Petersburg's Own Story of the Struggle for Justice and Democracy* (New York, 1991). See also his lecture "On the Role of Lawyers in the Building of a State Committed to the Rule of Law in the USSR and the Modern World," *The Advocate* (Northwestern University), Autumn 1990, pp. 7–10.

44. See James H. Billington, "Soviet Attitudes and Values: Prospects for the Future," published in *The USSR and the Sources of Soviet Policy*, Kennan Institute Occasional Paper no. 34, 1978, esp. pp. 106, 110; also published in the *Congressional Record* of the Senate October 14, 1978 (S 19396).

45. The couplet is itself the title of an article on the BBC in *Rossiiskaia Gazeta*, August 24, 1991, p. 4. Speaking of his isolation in Foros, where "everything was turned off," Gorbachev said, "We were able to catch some broadcasts and find out what was happening. We got BBC best of all—best of all BBC. They were the clearest signal. Radio Liberty, then Voice of America." Transcript in *New York Times*, August 23, 1991, p. A10.

46. Judgment offered by the correspondents compiling the excellent composite of eyewitness accounts, "Sobytiia, kotorye potriasli mir," in *Rossiiskaia*

Gazeta, August 23, 1991, p. 8. The role of the new electronic media is one of the most important and least studied aspects of this period. Both Russian commercial firms and a variety of Western interlocutors played important roles, but no one has assessed concrete influences and related them to the overall chronology of events. For a general statement, see John Hughes, "Moscow Witnesses an Information Revolution," *Christian Science Monitor,* August 29, 1991. For the continued functioning of Echo Moscow, see the short note by Evgeniia Pishchikova, "Delali vse, chtoby nichego ne delat," *Rossiiskaia Gazeta,* August 27, 1991, p. 4; and the detailed chronicle of the reporting, action, and thoughts of the staff of Echo Moscow during the three days: S. A. Buntman, S. L. Korzun et al., . . . *Deviatnadtsatoe, Dvadtsatoe, Dvadtsat pervoe . . . Svobodnoe radio dlia svobodnykh liudei,* Moscow, 1991. On the role of Russian television, see "Sdalas bez boia," *Trud,* November 11, 1991.

47. Alain Touraine saw the victory over the coup as the triumph of an aroused "democratic conscience" over the "hyperliberalism" that deifies the free market as the answer to all problems and is adopted in the economic sphere by a wide variety of authoritarian politicians from Pinochet to Deng Zhiaobing to the technocrats of the European community, whose diverse ranks the Soviet putschists presumably would have joined. See "Une leçon pour l'Europe," *Le Monde,* August 27, 1991, p. 5.

48. Concluding words of James H. Billington, "USSR: The Birth of a Nation," *Washington Post,* September 8, 1991, p. C2.

49. For a fuller discussion of Kalashnikov, see James H. Billington, "Keeping the Faith in the USSR After a Thousand Years," *Smithsonian,* April 1989, pp. 131–43, esp. pp. 135–36.

50. Aleksei Zuichenko, "Rezervny Sovmin v Bunkere," *Nezavisimaia Gazeta,* August 27, 1991, pp. 1, 4.

51. Andrei Karaulov, interview with Gennady Burbulis, *Nezavisimaia Gazeta,* September 5, 1991, p. 7.

52. Poll of 1,438 in Krasnoiarsk, St. Petersburg, Voronezh, and Lvov, reported in *Argumenty i Fakty,* August 1991, no. 33, p. 3.

53. For pictures and detailed biographies of Tiziakov and other putschists, see *Argumenty i Fakty,* August 1991, no. 33. p. 6.

54. Boris Pasternak, *Doctor Zhivago* (New York, 1958), p. 509.

55. *Ibid.,* p. 519.

56. Cited in Olga Zhmyreva and Igor Popov, "Byl v MGU Professor—Kovalev," *Vechernaia Moskva,* October 31, 1991, p. 2.

57. I discussed this apocalypticism in "Russia's Quest for Identity," *Washington Post,* January 21, 1990, p. B7. The importance of Aleksandr Kabakov's work amid this general mood was particularly well characterized in

Martin Walker, "Punk Perestroika," *New Republic*, December 4, 1989, pp. 22–27.

The tragedy at Chernobyl was widely accorded apocalpytical significance, particularly since the word also meant wormwood, and thus suggested to many the apocalyptical Star Wormwood from the Book of Revelation. In late May 1991, when I visited Leonid Leonov, the last great novelist of the early Soviet period still living at age ninety-two, he professed to be a devout believer and showed me the enormous manuscript on which he has been working for many years. It deals with the end of the world and is charged with religious symbolism. A small portion was published in *Novy Mir*, no. 11, 1984, pp. 6–19. It is discussed in V. A. Kovalev and N. A. Groznova, eds., *Leonid Leonov: Tvorcheskaia individualnost i literaturny protsess* (Leningrad, 1987), and a supplementary fragment is in *Moskva*, no. 5, 1989, pp. 3–19.

58. The official monthly of the Moscow Patriarchate published an entire issue on the martyred Patriarch Tikhon, who was canonized in October 1989 (*Russian Orthodox Readings*, no. 4, 1990), and a series of articles on St. Seraphim and the Diveevo convent (*ibid.*, nos. 1, 3, 1990), usefully discussed in Oxana Antic, "The Russian Orthodox Church Moves Towards Coming to Terms with Its Past," *Report on the USSR*, Radio Liberty, March 8, 1991, pp. 4–6.

The prophecies of Seraphim are based largely on manuscripts seen by a Russian emigré, Ivan M. Andreev, in Sarov and Diveevo in 1926 just before the monstery was shut. See *Pravednik vo veki zhivet: K desiatiletiiu so dnia prestavleniia prep. Serafima Sarovskago 1903–1953* (Jordanville, N.Y.: Holy Trinity Monastery, 1953), pp. 58–73. For a different version recently recovered from the papers of Father Paul Florensky, apparently based on the earlier collection of Sergei Nilun, see text and commentary in *Literaturnaia Ucheba*, Book 1, 1991, pp. 131–34. Seraphim's prophecies were apparently preserved by both Florensky and the art restorer Yu. A. Olsufev. They worked together in the monastery at Zagorsk and perished together in the gulag at Solovetsk. Seraphim's prophecies have been hailed by the reactionary as well as the democratic side of the Orthodox revival. See *Literaturny Irkutsk*, April 1990, edited by Valentin Rasputin. Praise of Seraphim was the only subject in a long series of speeches that elicited applause from Metropolitan Pitirim, like Rasputin a sympathizer with the putsch, at the opening meeting of the Congress of Compatriots on the first day of the coup.

59. Metropolitan Cyril explained to me in the course of our joint panel discussion before the Central Committee of the World Council of Churches at Geneva in September 1991 that the hierarchy of the Church

had agreed among themselves, when some of their members first entered into the revived parliamentary life of the USSR in the late 1980s, not to rise for symbolic political purposes. He explained that they were following that principle in the meeting, even though he and Juvenaly were already committed with the Patriarch to opposing the coup. Thus, three of the four top prelates of the Church resident in Moscow appear to have opposed the putsch, and their position was formally endorsed by the Synod of the Church that was convened on August 30. No public statement that I am aware of, however, was issued before late on the twentieth, and there are continued accusations that the decision to speak out came only then.

60. Carbon copy in LC of the original document, published text along with other church documents and Yeltsin's letter to the Patriarch in *Put*, no. 7/10, 1991, p. 2.

61. Sidorenko, *Tri dnia*, pp. 31, 59.

62. Father Viacheslav Polosin, "Uderzhivaiushchy teper," *Put*, no. 8/11, 1991, p. 5.

63. "Poslanie Patriarkha Moskovskogo i Vseia Rusi Aleksiia II," *Izvestiia*, August 24, 1991, p. 3.

64. "Komu davat sviatogo Georgiia? Barrikadnaia Mozaika," *Put*, no. 7/10, 1991, p. 3.

65. Abuladze's great film appears to have played an important role in the evolution toward reform of Gorbachev's Foreign Minister, Eduard Shevardnadze, who had earlier used his authority in Georgia to save the film from destruction. See his "Which Road Leads to the Cathedral?" in his *The Future Belongs to Freedom* (New York, 1991), esp. pp. 171–73.

   Gorbachev seems to have been less interested in the filmmaker. When I introduced Gorbachev to Abuladze at a state dinner during the Moscow summit in June 1988, Gorbachev showed no sign of recognition, and Abuladze said it was the first time they had ever met.

66. The early history and recent restoration of the monastery is described with ample illustration by Vadim Borisov in *Nashe Nasledie*, no. IV, 1988, pp. 54–67. An invaluable study written by a scholarly priest and frequent visitor to Optina in its last prerevolutionary days is Sergei Chetverikov, *Optina Pustyn* (Paris, 1926).

67. Pilar Bonet, "Poslednee Interviu o. Aleksandra Menia," *Panorama*, no. 13, 1990, p. 2. The anonymous study "Protoierei Aleksandr Men, kak kommentator Biblii," in an undated issue of *Troitsky Blagovestnik*, illustrates the vehemence of some clerical opposition to Men. The examination of different theories about the murder by Sergei Bychkov, "Khronika neraskrytogo Ubiistva," *Moskovsky Komsomolets*, October 25, 1991, p. 2,

leaves little doubt that the murder was well planned and politically or ideologically inspired.

68. Like many extreme nationalists, Zhirinovsky was born and raised on the periphery of empire, in Kazakhstan. His bizarre views and bizarre entourage are succinctly discussed by Wendy Sloane in *Moscow Magazine*, April–May 1992, pp. 40–47.

69. "Putsch 2" was the theme of Aleksei Uliukaev, "Pora perevorotov: Vstupaem li my v nee?" *Moskovskie Novosti*, September 15, 1991, p. 7, and was the title of an entire issue of the same publication in October. See also Michael Dobbs, "Moscow's New Worry: A 'December Putsch'," *Washington Post*, December 6, 1991, pp. A47–A49.

70. Afanasev, the head of the State Historical–Archival Institute in Moscow, which has now been incorporated into a much larger Russian State Humanistic (*Gumanitarny*) University, which he also heads, particularly attacks the selling of distribution rights to foreign commercial firms in his "Proizvol v obrashchenii s obshchestvennoi pamiatiu nedopustim," *Izvestiia*, March 9, 1992.

71. The computer program used in the parliament to determine the basic political orientation of deputies in the Russian Congresses changed its key criteria for assessing votes after the failed coup attempt from preferences for conservatism or reformism to partiality toward executive or legislative power.

72. Particularly devastating has been the allegation that about 20 percent of the church hierarchy (including a number of metropolitans) were known under code names by the Fifth Directorate of the KGB and were on specific occasions utilized and manipulated for political purposes at home and abroad. See the interview with Gleb Yakunin, "Abbat vykhodit na sviaz," *Argumenty i Fakty*, no. 1, 1992; the article of another priest who heads the committee of the Russian parliament on freedom of conscience, Viacheslav Polosin, "Vechny Rab ChK," *Izvestiia*, January 23, 1992, p. 3; and Aleksandr Nezhny, "Trete Imia," *Ogonek*, January 25–February 1, 1992. More details are provided by Yakunin in the stenographic report of the commission on the putsch of the Russian parliament: *O roli repressirovannykh organov v gosudarstvennom perevorote 19–21 avgusta 1991 g.*, February 4, 1992, pp. 94–102. This selective use of raw archival material has been criticized by some reformers like Afanasev as well as by reactionaries.

73. Gorbachev acknowledged that the absence of "the necessary coordination between the dismantling of the old structures . . . and the creation of new structures" was a tragic failing of his rule and "my fault as president." See

his interview of March 8, 1992, with Radio Liberty editors in Munich in RFE/RL Research Report, March 20, 1992, p. 55.

74. The interrogations of Kriuchkov on August 22 and of Pavlov on August 30 were published in *Der Speigel*, October 7, 1991, and translated and reprinted in *Avgust-91*, pp. 262–71.

75. This report by V. Anpilov, V. Yakushev, and I. Ebersvalde was published in *Molniia*, no. 24, in "*Chto Delat?*" no. 11, and in a special undated issue of *Literaturnaia Sibir* under the title "Avgustovsky putch: Koroli i shesterki provokatsii."

76. In fact, the interview by Iuliia Pospelova with General Kobets cited in this study indicates that the general had been making at least some rudimentary plans for resistance since November 1990 and had some kind of advanced understanding with nine other senior military figures. See "General bez armii, no s ideiami," *Sobesednik*, no. 37, 1991, p. 5.

77. The special issue of *Nasha Rossiia*, no. 19, 1991, includes interviews with the young soldier, Nikolai Bulichev, "Begushchy Fakel," and with Lieutenant General L. Zolotov, "Prikazov na shturm ne bylo . . . ?" (both by A. Golovenko), as well as with Captain Sergei Surovikin, "Zapadnia na sadovom." See also the spirited defense of one of the military leaders of the putsch, General Valentin Varennikov, by his son, Valery, "Nikogda ne otrekus ot svoego ottsa," *Nasha Rossiia*, no. 24, 1991, pp. 2–3, also by A. Golovenko, a writer for *Pravda* with a sideline of interviewing admirers of the putsch.

78. Interview of Alksnis by Vladmir Ivanov headed "Kogda liudei veli v gazovye kamery, oni nadeialis, chto ikh vedut mytsia v baniu," *Krasnoiarskaia Gazeta*, December 19, 1991, p. 1.

79. Description provided by the Russian historian Stepan Volk, formerly of the Marx-Engels-Lenin Institute, who wrote a remarkable article about me, explaining the political motivation of earlier criticisms of my work in *Bibliotekar*, no. 7, 1991, pp. 76–78.

   A recent articulation of Shafarevich's views is his "Rossiia naedine s soboi" in a special edition of *Literaturnaia Sibir* titled "Avgustovsky putch," pp. 3–4.

80. *Avgust-91*, p. 24.

81. See Sergei Platonov, *Ocherki po istorii smuty v Moskovskom Gosudarstve XVI-XVII vv* (Moscow, 1937), pp. 143–44, for a concise statement of his conception. For an English translation of a condensed version of this work by John Alexander, see *The Time of Troubles: A Historical Study of the Internal Crisis and Social Struggle in Sixteenth and Seventeenth Century Muscovy* (Lawrence, Kans., 1970). *Time of Troubles* is the title of the remarkable diary of the 1917–22 period by Platonov's friend and col-

league, Yury Gote, the historian and former director of the Rumiantsev Museum (later the Lenin Library), edited and translated by Terence Emmons (Princeton, 1988).

Use of the term "Time of Troubles" (in capital letters without explanation) has become commonplace even in the West for describing the current period in Soviet history. See, for instance, John Morrison, "The Bolshevik Who Came in from the Cold," *Los Angeles Times Magazine*, October 6, 1991, p. 41. Russians often simply use the word *smuta*, as in the headline on the edition of the official bulletin reporting on Yeltsin's new economic program: "Bolshaia Smuta ili Veliky perelom?" *Kurer sezda narodnykh deputatov RSFSR*, no. 18, (November 1, 1991), p. 1. See also the interview with the writer Boris Vasilev, "Perezhit by Rossii chetvertuiu smutu," *Prolog*, no. 14, 1992, pp. 8–9.

82. Discussion by the Vice Chairman of the Commission, Vladimir Yudin, reported in the Associated Press article by Alan Cooperman, "Coup Investigators: December Looks a Lot Like August," December 27, 1991.

83. Text of Moscow Russian Television account of Russian Federation Supreme Soviet Session of December 27 in FBIS-SOV-91-250, December 30, 1991, p. 41.

84. *Ibid.*, and "Russian Coup Investigators Suffer Two Setbacks," Reuters Library Report, December 27, 1991.

85. Cooperman, "Coup Investigators," cites Aleksandr Obolensky, head of the commission, as implicating Nazarbaev; Moscow INTERFAX of December 27 says that Nazarbaev refused to support one statement by the coup organizers, FBIS-SOV-91-250, December 30, 1991, p. 9. See also the Vesti newscast "Key Leaders Implicated in Putsch," broadcast on December 27 and reprinted on the same page of FBIS.

There were persistent rumors in December that Gorbachev had bargained successfully prior to resigning as President of the Union against any personal liability to prosecution, the expectation being that many of the defendants would implicate him in some way. In the course of a guarded and sophisticated self-defense put forward by several junta members in an interview from prison on March 27 by the Moscow TV program "Vzgliad," Baklanov flatly declared: "Gorbachev was the organizer of these events." FBIS-USR-92-039, April 18, 1992, p. 4.

86. An extraordinarily detailed five-page "plan of action" for the Communist Party faction in the Russian parliament to remove Yeltsin legally from power on March 28 was discovered by the commission of the Russian Parliament investigating the coup attempt. *Plan Deistvii–28*, in LC.

87. Text of secret telegram from N. Sapozhnikov, First Secretary of the Communist Party of the Udmurt Autonomous Republic, in Izhevsk, to Oleg

Baklanov in his capacity as a member of the State Committee on the Extraordinary Situation, with a copy sent to O. S. Shenin in his capacity as Secretary of the Central Committee of the Soviet Communist Party, August 19, 9:45 P.M., in LC.

Shenin had, in effect, replaced Gorbachev as First Secretary of the Party during the coup attempt. Piotr Korotkevich, one of the USSR's top missile scientists, identified Baklanov as the key figure behind the putsch in an interview detailing the extravagant corruption of the military–industrial complex that Baklanov in many ways dominated. See Yury Shchekochikhin, "Putch, novaia versiia," *Literaturnaia Gazeta*, October 2, 1991, p. 3.

88. This document is printed in full in *O roli repressirovannykh organov*, pp. 34–36. Translation by Harry Leich.

Yanaev's inebriation was the central theme of Peter Gumbel's early report, "How Not to Mount a Coup: The Lessons from the Kremlin," *Wall Street Journal*, August 29, 1991, pp. 1, A6, based on the testimony of Gorbachev loyalists who remained within the Kremlin. This account, with all its colorful, semicomical detail, may have helped inculcate in the minds of many in the West the view that persists to this day that the entire effort was not altogether serious.

89. The text was published in *Rossiiskaia Gazeta*, October 11, 1991, pp. 3–6, with an excellent explanation of its genesis and philosophy on page 7. Its formal submission to the parliament was postponed to avoid distraction from the economic reforms, and at least four other versions have subsequently been put forth (including one by Anatoly Sobchak). See the discussion by A. Sobchak and S. Alekseev in *Izvestiia*, nos. 75, 76, 1992, and the answer by Vladimir Lafitsky in *Izvestiia*, no. 83, 1992, p. 3.

90. Andrei Novikov, "Armiia v roli partii," *Vek XX i Mir*, no. 8, 1991, p. 19.

91. See the penetrating analysis of a people's deputy, Vladimir Rebrikov, in *O roli repressirovannykh organov*, February 4, 1992, p. 94.

92. Aleksandr Prokhanov, "Zametki konservatora," *Nash Sovremennik*, no. 8, 1990, as cited in Novikov, "Armiia," p. 17.

93. For a good early account, see Justin Burke, "Attempted Coup Galvanizes Russia's Youth," *Christian Science Monitor*, August 27, 1991. For the totally new perspective of the youngest generation of Russian journalists, see David Remnick, "Letter from Moscow," *The New Yorker*, March 23, 1992, pp. 65–68.

94. Geoffrey Hosking, "The Outlook for a Democratic Russia," *Report on the USSR*, October 11, 1991, p. 2. I draw on this excellent short account of the origins of the democratic movement, reprinted with a series of conference papers from September 19–20, 1991, under the rubric, "Nation-

alism and Self-Determination in the Republics: The Russian Revival."

95. For characterizations of the parties (without the comparisons here suggested), see Eberhard Schneider, "The New Political Forces in Russia, Ukraine, and Belorussia," *Report on the USSR*, December 13, 1991, pp. 10–11.

96. Valentin Rasputin, "Posle sobytii, nakanune sobytii," *Sovetskaia Rossiia*, January 23, 1992, p. 4, and his desperate appeal at least to restore the unity of "the three-headed Siamese twin" of Russia, Ukraine, and Belorus: "Chto dalshe, bratia-slaviane?" *Den*, April 5–11, 1992, p. 5.

97. Vladimir Turbin described the new Soviet man as an "epic knight charging forth across the steppe on a horse called Proletarian Strength, bearing in his heart the image of a beautiful Helen called Rosa Luxemburg." "Proshchai, epos!" *Literaturnaia Gazeta*, June 6, 1990, p. 4.

98. See, in addition to materials cited in note 72, two highly critical journalistic articles about the two metropolitans known to have been most sympathetic with the putsch, Pitirim and Filaret of Kiev, by, respectively, Mikhail Pozdniaev, "Okromia ego Arkhiereistva," *Stolitsa*, no. 26, 1991, pp. 4–7, and Aleksandr Nezhny, "Ego Blazhenstvo bez Mitry i Zhezla," *Ogonek*, no. 48, 1991, pp. 8–10, and no. 49, pp. 20–22.

99. See two interview articles on Lubenchenko: "Deputatskaia 'Razbora'," *Smena*, no. 12, 1991, pp. 56–62, and "Naedine so vsemi," *Moskovskie Novosti*, no. 51, 1991.

100. Gleb Pavlovsky, "Sudba Rossii," *Nezavisimaia Gazeta*, November 11, 1991, p. 5.

101. *Deviatnadtsatoe* . . . , p. 5.

102. "Svecha Rossii," *Rossiiskaia Gazeta*, April 1, 1992, p. 2.

103. Metropolitan Cyril of Smolensk and Kaliningrad, "O Vlastekh i Voinstve," *Moskovsky Tserkovny Vestnik*, February 1992, p. 12.

104. See the open letter to the Patriarch signed by the notoriously antireligious Academician B. A. Rybakov and five others in *Russky Vestnik*, April 1–8, 1992, p. 3.

105. Leonid Monchinsky's *Proshchenoe Voskresene* (*Absolution Sunday*, the last Sunday before Lent) was finished in 1982, was published in Germany in 1989, and began to be serialized in *Literaturnaia Ucheba*, Book 1, 1991, pp. 4–39. His next work, *Chernaia Svecha* (*The Black Candle*), is scheduled to appear in 1992 and will apparently deal with the link between crime and the Communist elite, the problem of the Soviet "mafia."

106. This creates an attitude that "does not so much work up hatred toward temptation as fall in love with overcoming it." Viktor Trostnikov, "Voskresenie cherez Proshchenie," *Literaturnaia Ucheba*, Book 1, 1991, p. 3.

"We ask only repentance and cleansing [*pokaianiia i ochishcheniia*]," said Gleb Yakunin in his indictment of the Church hierarchy's past connections with the KGB, *O roli repressirovannykh organov*, February 4, 1992, p. 101. The theme of repentance spilled out into the popular journals. See Mikhail Pozdniaev, "Posle 'Pokaianiia'," *Stolitsa*, no. 20, 1991, pp. 37–39, and Nikolai Malinin, "Ishchu sponsora dlia pokaianiia," *Stolitsa*, no. 4, 1992, pp. 29–30.

107. Cited in Lynn Eliason, *Perestroika of the Russian Soul: Religious Renaissance in the Soviet Union* (Jefferson, N.C., 1991), p. 128.

108. Cited in Philip Yancy, "Praying with the KGB," *Christianity Today*, January 13, 1992, p. 18.

109. The term is used to describe the secret thirteen-man Holy Synod. Mikhail Frankov, "Zagadki sviashchennogo sinoda," *Moskovskie Novosti*, February 9, 1992, p. 24.

110. Trostnikov kindly gave me the text of his interview with Zinon, "Otkrovenny razgovor v monasheskoi kele," prior to publication, in LC.

111. From the transcript *Uchastie rukovodiashchiego sostava*, February 18, 1992, p. 86.

112. On young Yakovlev and young Budenny, see Loory, *Seven Days*, p. 141.

113. Cited from Likhachev, *Sobytiia 18–21 Avgusta 1991 g.*, p. 7.

114. Oleg Borodin, *Mikhail Gorbachev (Vzgliad iz oppozitsii)* (Moscow, 1991), pp. 111–6. This characterization of the August events was added by this member of the original liberal opposition to Gorbachev to his important and detailed account of Gorbachev's reactionary turn late in 1990. Borodin uses the relatively archaic word *spontanno* for spontaneous, perhaps in order to avoid using the more common term *stikhiino* which bore the burden of Leninist caricature.

115. Introduction to the Echo Moscow publication, . . . *Deviatnadtsatoe*, p. 5.

116. I have modified the English translation of Rozanov made by Vladimir Zviglianich in his stimulating unpublished work, "The Seduction of Autarky: Russia and the 'Unique Path'," pp. 34–35.

117. Kurt Campbell noted at the time that "the first visual scene the West saw on the morning of August 19" involved "an elderly babushka" lecturing a soldier in a tank that the move against Moscow was "morally wrong, you should be ashamed!" "Glasnost Shines in the Midst of the Moscow Coup," *Christian Science Monitor*, August 21, 1991, p. 19.

118. Zviglianich, "Seduction," p. 34.

119. *Ibid.*

120. Characterizations of the comparably defining moments of the equally unexpected Czech breakthrough to new beginnings in the mass gatherings

at Letná Stadium and Wenceslas Square in November 1989, by one of the heroes of those events, the young priest Václav Maly, in an interview in Augustin Hedberg, *Faith Under Fire and the Revolutions in Eastern Europe* (Princeton, N.J., 1992), pp. 13, 14, 11.

121. Cited from his oral presentation at a conference in the Vatican in January 1992, where he traced how the reform Communists' "revolution from above" led to a "revolution of conscience from below" that rendered traditional class warfare categories irrelevant and put Russia "on the threshold of a new civilization."

122. Cited in Victor Cohn, "Releasing the Power of Hope," *Washington Post Health*, June 2, 1992, pp. 10–11.

Index

INDEX

INDEX